Retriever Training Drills for Marking

JAMES B. SPENCER

Alpine
Blue Ribbon Books
Loveland, Colorado

Retriever Training Drills for Marking
Copyright© 2001 by James B. Spencer

Library of Congress Cataloging-in-Publication Data

Spencer, James B.
    Retriever training drills for marking / James B. Spencer.
        p. cm.
    ISBN 1-57779-032-4
    1. Retrievers--Training. I. Title.

SF429.R4 S629 2001
636.752'735--dc21   2001022722

Cover Photo: Theresa Spencer
Photos: James B. and Theresa Spencer
Editing: B. J. McKinney
Layout: Sharon Anderson
Cover Design: Laura Claassen

This book is available at special quantity discounts for breeders and for club promotions, premiums, or educational use. Write for details.

First printing October 2001

1 2 3 4 5 6 7 8 9 0

Printed in the United States of America.

Table of Contents

To Nancy Nieratko, who first suggested such a book—and then kept reminding me of it.

Preface

This book is a companion to *Retriever Training Drills for Blind Retrieves*. If you've already read that book, you can skip over to Chapter 2 and get ready to work on marking. But for those of you who are beginning with this book, perhaps I should explain the *raison d'être* for this multiple birth, especially to long-time readers of my work.

Frankly, at one time I thought I had already written all the retriever books I should. *Training Retrievers for Marshes & Meadows* explains how to train a retriever from puppyhood to finished dog status. *Retriever Training Tests* explains how to set up appropriate tests for training retrievers. And *Hunting Retrievers: Hindsights, Foresights, and Insights* describes the various retriever breeds and retriever dog-games. What else could one possibly say about retrievers? Nothing, I thought.

Then, a few years ago, I met Nancy Nieratko at a seminar I conducted in New Jersey. During lunch, and again at supper that evening—she and several other attendees dined with my wife and me—she bemoaned how difficult it is for a beginner to take a retriever from the Junior level to the Senior level in AKC hunting tests for retrievers. She told me that I should write a book to be titled *Getting to Senior*. Throughout these lamentations and entreaties, she used the word "drill" in almost every sentence. She mentioned, by name, many drills people use to advance their dogs, and pointed out that information about them is passed mostly by word of mouth, with almost nothing written down. Most beginners, she insisted, have no way to find out about these drills, at least at first. Further, she stressed, most beginners don't understand how necessary drilling—repetition, repetition, and more repetition—is for successful retriever training.

That rang a bell with me. In fact, a similar situation in the area of test design motivated my first book, *Retriever Training Tests*. But, like most writers, I instinctively resist book suggestions from others. So I gave Nancy my standard response: "If you think such a book should be written, why don't you write it yourself?" She demurred, saying she wasn't much of a writer, then went on to insist that such a book needed to be written.

By the time my wife and I were again home, I had all but dismissed the idea. I couldn't dispute Nancy's arguments, but I had no enthusiasm for such a project. Within a couple of weeks, I received a note from Nancy thanking me for the seminar—and again suggesting this book. "No way," I thought, "too much work!" (Someone long ago described writing a book as the "hardest work there is that doesn't involve heavy lifting.") Nancy and I repeated this stimulus/response sequence several times through the following few years, especially around holidays. She would send a card with a note suggesting the book. In a most non-Pavlovian way, my responses gradually weakened.

At length, I was "done in" by the enthusiasm of another woman, Joanne Carriera, who lives in Colorado and has never heard of Nancy Nieratko. In mid-1998, while she was doing an interview for a website for Alpine Publications, Inc., Joanne phoned me for information about myself and my books. After getting all the basic information, she asked—quite off-handedly, mostly to end the conversation politely—whether I had any ideas for future books. To my utter amazement, I heard myself blurting out, "Why, yes; I've been thinking of doing one about retriever training drills!"

With most website types—who, quite frankly, don't know which end of a dog to feed and which to clean up after—that would have passed almost unnoticed. However, Joanne is that rare website type who also "does" dogs. In fact, she has been heavily involved with herding dogs for years. Herding dog trainers drill their dogs as much as or perhaps even more than retriever trainers. (In fact, we "borrowed" the blind retrieve from herding trials.) So, the word "drills" clicked with her. She started asking intriguing questions, which I struggled to answer. We talked at length. Through this discussion, her contagious enthusiasm—for *any* book that would describe appropriate drills for beginners and convince them that they *must* drill their dogs—carried the day.

Next thing I knew I had a contract with Alpine to write a book to be titled *Retriever Training Drills*. Only after completing the second draft did I begin to suspect that I was working on two separate books. I wrote to Betty McKinney, Alpine's owner/publisher, saying, "I think I hear two heartbeats!" She studied my explanation and sent word to me through her Administrative Assistant, Sharon Anderson, that it was indeed twins and that I should proceed accordingly. Thus, *Retriever Training Drills* became *Retriever Training Drills for Marking* and *Retriever Training Drills for Blind Retrieves*.

THESE BOOKS ARE "AUXILIARY" TEXTS

Like *Retriever Training Tests*, these two books should supplement a complete training manual, such as *Training Retrievers for Marshes and Meadows*. The *Tests* book focuses on how to set up effective tests while following the *Marshes and Meadows* program. These two new books, *Drills for Marking* and *Drills for Blind Retrieves*, focus on the specific drills to use while following the *Marshes and Meadows* program.

THESE BOOKS EXPLAIN WHY

Like *Marshes and Meadows* and *Tests*, these two books tell you not only how, but also why.

When I started out in retrievers—back when the Roman Senator, Cato, was ending every speech with *"Carthago delenda est!"* (Carthage must be destroyed!)—I irritated several pros and not a few experienced amateurs with my incessant question, "Why should I do it that way?" I was seeking information, but they took my question as a challenge to the worth of whatever processes they were recommending. I've found that people who are totally wrapped up in dog training, especially of the "labor-intensive" retriever variety, tend to suffer a "process-oriented" form of tunnel blindness. They think only in terms of *how*, with little or no consideration of *why*. Of course, in anything as complex as retriever training, just figuring out the myriad of *how*'s is a daunting task. Consequently, retriever trainers, and especially pros, waste little of their time speculating about the associated *why*'s.

Frankly, that comes from long years of working with dogs, and therefore focussing entirely on canine mental processes. Pros can teach dogs only *how* to do this or that. They can't explain to dogs *why* they should do it. Would that it were otherwise! For example, it would be so nice if, before force-breaking a dog, a person could sit down with the beast and explain both what he is to do and why he needs this particular skill. You know, like you can do with a child. But dogs have nothing remotely approaching human intelligence.

People, on the other hand, are never completely comfortable with knowing only *how*. Rational intelligence craves information about *why*. In fact, curiosity about *why* starts at or before two years of age and continues until death. You may have heard the story about the man and his seven-year-old son walking down the street. The boy asked one question after another:

"Why is the sky up?" ... "Why can't penguins fly?" ... "Why does it snow only in winter?" ... and so on. To each question, his father answered, "Beats me. I just don't know." Eventually, the boy asked, "Daddy, do you mind me asking all these questions?" The father replied, "Of course not, son. If you don't ask questions, how can you ever learn anything?"

Back when I started in retrievers, I often felt like that kid. I'd ask why, and get no answer, beyond an angry "Because it works!" By and large, I've had to work out my own *why*'s over the years—which has sometimes been a struggle. Thus, in my writing, I've always tried to share that information with my readers. I look at it this way: I write *about* dogs, but dogs can't read, so I must write *for* people—and people want to know *why*.

THESE BOOKS FOCUS ON FIELD WORK

Marshes and Meadows covers all phases of retriever training: puppy training, basic obedience, single marks, force-breaking, double marks, basic blind retrieves, advanced marks and blinds. Although each training phase requires drills of some kind, I've limited the drills in these two supplemental books to those involved in actual field work: single marks, double marks, triple marks, and blind retrieves. To keep these books reasonable in size, I've omitted the drills associated with puppy training, obedience, and force-breaking, all of which have received extensive coverage in many other texts. Not so field work drills. As Nancy Nieratko pointed out, most field drills are passed along by word of mouth, but have never been written down. Such written material as may exist is scattered through many sources, mostly magazine articles. Thus, in these two books, I've tried to bring together for the first time a comprehensive (although admittedly not exhaustive) collection.

THESE BOOKS ARE FOR AMATEURS
TRAINING THEIR OWN DOGS

In justice, I should point out that, in all likelihood, field trial pros developed almost every drill in this book. All of us who enjoy field work with retrievers owe practically everything we have—in the breeds themselves, in training techniques and equipment, and in basic dog-game formats—to field trialers, especially the highly talented and hard-working pros who have contributed so much, not only to field trials, but also to all other areas of retrieverdom.

However, in orienting this book to amateurs training their own dogs, I have necessarily had to focus on hunters and hunt test participants, not field trialers. Most hunters and over half of all hunt testers train their own dogs. This is not the case among field trialers. Very few amateur field trialers train their own dog. By "field trialers," I mean those who compete seriously and successfully in the major stakes, where championship points are awarded to the placing dogs. Field trials are so competitive that, for most participants, full-time professional training is the only rational road to success. Granted, a handful of wealthy amateurs who have unlimited leisure time and extensive training facilities do indeed train their own retrievers well enough to compete with the pros. (I do not include in this group those somewhat more numerous amateurs who "train their own dogs" under the direct and constant supervision of pros. By any reasonable standard, their dogs receive full-time professional training.) Thus, as I said, very few amateur field trialers train their own dogs. So writing a *training* book for field trialers would be foolish. (An appropriate book for aspiring field trialers would contain only a list of the names, addresses, and phone numbers of all the field trial pros across the country. That's all the information the novice field trialer needs—and the sooner he gets it, the sooner he will begin to win.) Since I've written this book for the hunter and hunt tester, not the field trialer, I've omitted those few drills that have little application outside of the esoteric field trial world.

Throughout this book, I've kept in mind the limitations under which most amateurs must train their own dogs for hunting and hunting tests. Few have ideal training grounds. Few have unlimited time. Few have unlimited discretionary spending money for equipment. Frankly, keeping such limits in mind has been easy, for I've been drilling my own dogs under similar circumstances for several decades! I would have had difficulty *not* identifying with all other such trainers!

REPETITIO
EST MATER
STUDIORUM

1
Why Drill?

I've been told that angels have what is called "infused knowledge." That term presumably means that they received all the knowledge they have—which I've been told is considerable, at least when compared to that of human beings—without effort. They didn't have to memorize definitions and principles. They didn't have to work a seemingly endless series of problems. In fact, they didn't have to study in any way. They just *know*, period.

I've had no personal experience with angels, so I can only repeat here what I've heard about them. But I have had extensive experience with dogs over the past 45 years, and I have observed that dogs, too, have "infused knowledge" in a limited way. We breed them to do certain things naturally or, as we often say, instinctively. Hounds trail and tree fur naturally. Pointing breeds seek and point birds naturally. Spaniels quarter and flush birds naturally. Retrievers mark falls and retrieve naturally. And so on. Dogs do these things—and the above is by no means an exhaustive list of instinctive behaviors we have bred into the various types of dogs—with only the most elementary exposure to suitable opportunities. Given half a chance, nature will out.

Useful as these instinctive behaviors are to those of us who enjoy hunting with dogs, they are not sufficient in and of themselves to produce finished workers. Far from it. To turn a well-bred dog into the kind of worker we seek, we must complement his instinctive behavior with appropriate elements of "learned behavior," a.k.a. "training." How much training a given dog requires depends on what type he is and on how "polished" the boss wants him to be. Hounds require—and will accept—very little. If a hound avoids running trash, loads up on command, and comes in when called (provided he has nothing better to do), he's "well trained." Dogs from long-tailed pointing breeds (the Pointer and the three Setter breeds) require more training. They should maintain some sort of contact with their handlers, should be staunch on point (and perhaps steady to wing and shot), should back-point, should stop-to-flush, and should respond to basic obedience commands (*Whoa, Come, Heel*) under reasonable circumstances. For owners who insist on retrieving, they should also be force-broken. Dogs of the bob-tailed pointing breeds (the German Shorthair, Brittany, Weimaraner, Vizsla, German Wirehair, Wirehaired Pointing Griffon, and so on) require even more training than long-tailed pointing dogs, especially in range control and retrieving (which may or may not be natural to them). Dogs of the flushing spaniel breeds (English Springer, English Cocker, American Cocker, Welsh Springer, Clumber, Sussex, American Water Spaniel, and so on) require substantially more training than bob-tailed pointing breeds. They must quarter within gun range, turn on a whistle command, flush vigorously, and retrieve very well (which most of them do naturally) on land and in water. Ideally a spaniel should be steady, that is, it should *Hup* (sit) after flushing a bird, and remain in place until sent to retrieve or continue hunting. As you can see, as we move from hounds to pointing breeds to spaniels, the training requirements increase dramatically.

When we move from spaniels to retrievers, well, as Al Jolson used to say, "You ain't seen nothin' yet!" The training requirements for retrievers is at least an order of magnitude (ten times) greater than that of spaniels! A retriever must sit quietly by the blind until all the birds are down. He must ignore decoys. He must do multiple marked retrieves through all manner of natural hazards (wind direction, cover variations, terrain changes, and so forth). And, most importantly, he must do blind retrieves on land and in water. Nothing in the instincts of any dog inclines him to do blind retrieves naturally. Thus, the blind retrieve is totally trained, totally taught, as a complex mixture of three basic elements: lining, stopping, and casting. Although the blind retrieve alone makes retriever training much more "labor intensive" than spaniel training, the rest of retriever field training—namely, marked retrieving—also requires a lot of work, at least as much as it takes to fully train a spaniel. This book covers drills with which you can bring out your retriever's basic marking instincts and instill adequate control on marked retrieves. (The companion volume, *Retriever Training Drills for Blind Retrieves*, covers drills for blinds.)

But before getting into the drills themselves, you should acquaint yourself with the underlying motivation for drilling as such. Only after you understand that can you maximize the benefits of the drills described in this book.

FOR PEOPLE: "REPETITIO EST MATER STUDIORUM"
(*"Repetition is the Mother of Learning Techniques"*)

This Latin proverb is traditionally mistranslated as "repetition is the mother of learning." Through dint of—you guessed it—repetition, this mistranslation has become widely accepted in our culture. It even rings with profound wisdom—because it is pithy, because it deals in some abstract way with "learning," and, of course, because it has been repeated so often.

Be that as it may, "repetition is the mother of learning" misses the point of this old Roman proverb—by mistranslating *"studiorum"* as "learning" instead of as some more accurate term, such as "studies," "efforts," "approaches," or (most accurate, in this particular case) "learning techniques." For the ancient Romans, this proverb proclaimed that, without repetition, no *approach* to learning could be effective. Although true for both physical and mental skills, it is more obviously so for the former. To acquire any physical skill, one must practice, practice, practice. In any sport, different coaches break their practice sessions down in different ways, but they all insist on seemingly endless repetitions of drills. In the early 1970s (as I recall), psychologists developed a new approach to the acquisition of physical skills, namely, "mental practice." In this technique, the student closes his eyes and visualizes mentally that he is performing the skill properly, and also visualizes the results. For example, a golfer pictures himself swinging a 5-iron correctly, and then visualizes the ball climbing crisply before falling on the green. Various experiments indicated that this could be 70 to 80 percent as effective as physical practice. Did this new learning technique sidestep, and therefore disprove, *"repetitio est mater studiorum"*? No way! Essential to the success of "mental practice" is, you guessed it, repetition! The person must repeat this exercise over and over for about 15 minutes each session, for several sessions a day, for several days before showing the promised improvement. (And, of course, he would improve still more if he spent the same amount of time hitting real golf balls.)

The acquisition of mental skills also requires repetition. Whether in mathematics, a physical science, a social science, a philosophic discipline, or whatever, the general learning process consists of the same two phases: The student learns and memorizes the basic definitions, principles, and methodologies; then he applies these to a series of "problems" (equations, experiments, situations, syllogisms, and so forth). Repetition is essential for both memorization and problem solving. Educators are forever developing (and abandoning) new approaches, new ways to present the material in this or that discipline. But, to be even minimally successful, each new approach must rely heavily on repetitions by the students. Thus, in human learning, whether physical or mental skills are involved, we can confidently state that, to be effective, every learning technique must be lovingly nursed at the bountiful breasts of "Mother Repetition."

FOR DOGS: "EXERCITATIO EST MATER STUDIORUM"
(*"Drilling is the Mother of Training Techniques"*)

If repetition is essential for human learning, how could it be less than essential for dog training? Dogs, after all, lack human intelligence. (If you doubt that, try teaching a dog to read and write!) Contrary to today's trendy canine psycho-babble, we train dogs—we always have and always will—through a process which Pavlov long ago named "conditioning." We teach a dog to respond in a certain way to a certain stimulus—for example, to sit on a single whistle blast—by making sitting the dog's "conditioned response" to the whistle blast stimulus. We can condition a dog thusly through various training techniques, some positive, some negative, some more, and some less effective. But, essential to the success of whatever techniques we use is—again you guessed it—repetition, and lots of it!

In common dog-training parlance, frequent repetition of specific training techniques is called "drilling." Thus, we train dogs through drilling. We drill them to bring out their natural instincts, and we drill them to teach them to perform tasks beyond their natural instincts. Over the years, dog trainers have developed better and better techniques, frequently as a result of improvements in equipment. However, the one constant through the entire history of dog training is, and always will be, *drilling*.

Drills prepare a retriever for hunting tests.

TRIAL-AND-SUCCESS—TRIAL-AND-ERROR

In general, you use a two-phased approach to training your dog in any skill. In the first phase, which I have long called "trial-and-success," you lead your dog through the stimulus/response sequence under circumstances in which he has almost no chance to make a mistake. Let's take sitting on the whistle as an example. With your puppy on lead, you toot the whistle as you push his rump to the ground with your left hand and hold his head up with the lead. As soon as he is sitting, you praise him (very important). You do this repeatedly until he begins to sit before you can push his rump down. In this phase, you have led him through the proper response and you have rewarded him (with praise—or even food treats, if you like). He now knows how he should respond to the *Sit*-whistle, but he doesn't yet understand that he *must* do it every time.

To teach him the *necessity* of sitting on command, you move into phase two, which I have long called "trial-and-error," in which you allow him to make mistakes and correct him each time he does. With the puppy still on lead, so you can control him, you toot the whistle when he is a little distracted. If he sits, you praise him. If he ignores the whistle, you tap him crisply on the rump, either with your hand or a "sit-stick." Although this should not be a heavy blow, he should feel it and find it unpleasant enough to be avoided in the future. This tap on the rump puts him in a sitting position—so you praise him (even more important after a correction). You repeat this with various distractions to tempt him to ignore the whistle. Gradually, he learns that not sitting on the whistle brings unpleasant consequences—just as sitting on the whistle brings pleasant consequences. Eventually, after you have given him enough of this trial-and-error work, he will sit automatically when you toot the whistle, no matter what.

To put it another way: In the trial-and-success phase, you teach your dog to "do good," in the trial-and-error phase, you teach him to "avoid evil." To be fully conditioned, he needs both. Trial-and-success, because of its rewards, gives your dog a positive attitude toward whatever command you are teaching him. Trial-and-error, because of its punishments, teaches him that he must obey, whether he feels like it or not. Both phases are necessary to completely condition your dog.

In recent years, a lot of ink has been splashed about advocating "totally positive reinforcement." Loosely translated, this means use only phase-one techniques, with their rewards, but never use phase-two techniques, with their punishments. This is pure psycho-babble. When your retriever is high-balling after a jack rabbit instead of carrying your line to a blind retrieve—and especially if the rabbit is heading toward a four-lane divided—you'll be glad you reinforced the *Sit*-whistle with the "*not* totally positive reinforcements" of the trial-and-error phase. Had you used only the "totally positive reinforcement" of the trial-and-success phase, he would almost certainly decide to forego whatever delights you might have in store for him this time. He would rather catch the rabbit.

When your retriever is properly conditioned—to stop on the whistle, or obey any other command—he will obey happily, because of phase-one drilling, but he will also have some fear of disobeying, because of phase-two drilling. To be reliable, he needs both. As the ancient Romans said: "*Verba sapientibus*" (words for the wise).

DRILL, BUT DON'T OVERWORK YOUR DOG!

I have stressed the necessity of drilling so much because so many beginners have difficulty believing it's really necessary. They seem to think that as soon as the dog does something right once, he is fully trained in that particular area. "Hey, let's move on to something new and exciting! Why mess around with what he already knows?" I've had to deal with this attitude in many of the beginners I have helped out. I have heard it in the seminars I have conducted and in the ones I have attended. Other experienced trainers have told me of similar experiences. In fact, when I first began working on this book, I asked two people, one in New Jersey, the other in Kansas, what they would recommend I include. Both are well past the beginner stage now, but not so far removed from it that they don't remember it quite clearly. I expected that each of them would request that I include this or that special drill. To my surprise, neither of them mentioned a specific drill. Instead, both of them—independently, for they don't even know each other—urged me to do everything I could to convince beginners that drilling is absolutely necessary.

But, having put so much stress on the necessity of drilling, I now fear that I may lead a very small minority of beginners into the mistaken notion that they should drill their dogs spraddle-legged in every training session. I've known a few such beginners. They are very intense, totally focussed, and a joy to work with, for they absorb everything you tell them like sponges—and can repeat it back to you word for word months later if necessary. Most of them stay in the sport a long time and become excellent trainers. However, they tend to take too much out of their dogs for many years (and many dogs). They do this not by overly negative training techniques but simply by too much drilling per training session, day in, day out, week in, week out, for years. Whenever such a person gets a dog out of his crate, the dog knows he will be totally exhausted before he gets any kind of rest. The dog learns to adapt his pace to the workload he knows he is facing. Instead of running, he walks. And, strangely enough, if the dog walks straight enough, this type of beginner doesn't seem to notice how slowly he is moving. In short, his first few dogs become very precise "pigs." (A "pig" is a retriever with no style.)

So, for the minority of beginners with such tendencies, let me caution against too much drilling per session. Every dog has a "magic number" for repetitions. That number may be three or it may be eight, but it will seldom be anything greater than eight. In one training session, repeat a drill up to the dog's magic number and he will continue to improve, and will maintain his style. Push him beyond it and he will either deliberately mess up (especially Chesapeakes), or he will slow his pace. A few do both.

It's up to the trainer to know his dog's magic number—and to respect it! You can determine your dog's magic number by watching both his performance and his style. When he begins to do a drill worse instead of better, or when he begins to slow down, you should realize that you have exceeded his magic number. Put him up immediately, and next time you get him out, reduce the number of repetitions accordingly.

If possible, train with a group. In a group, you take turns working and resting your dogs, which reduces the risk of overworking any one of them in any one session. If you can't train with a group as often as you should, consider training two or three dogs, so you can rotate them. If you train alone and have only one dog, you simply have to put him up for a rest and a drink of water at appropriate intervals. This is extremely difficult to do, I know. When you are standing around with no one to talk to while your dog resets his magic number counter, time hangs heavily on your hands. But just grit your teeth and remember that you want a stylish retriever, not a pig.

THE DRILLS IN THIS BOOK

In a very technical sense, this book contains not drills, but training procedures. Only you can turn them into drills—by running your dog through them repetitively. If you were to use each one of them only once before moving on, you would not be drilling your dog, and he would end up thoroughly confused, not thoroughly trained. On the other hand, if you drill him appropriately with them, he should become a retriever you can be proud of, and he will enjoy the process as much as you do. It's up to you—not me, and not your dog.

Some of the drills in this book are phase one, trial-and-success drills, intended to help you lead your dog through the proper response with minimal chance of error. Some of them are phase two, trial-and-error drills, intended to tempt your dog to make a mistake so you can correct him. Some of them combine phase one and phase two, in that they start out as phase one and then advance into phase two. As you study each drill, you will see where it fits in this two-phased approach.

This book does not—and could not—contain every drill used by retriever trainers. Even if it contained all of them as of today, by tomorrow it would be missing a few, for trainers all over the country are developing new ones regularly. However, this book does contain a representative set of drills, certainly enough to train a retriever to do everything retrievers are supposed to do, at least according to hunting test standards. Incidentally, as best I can recall, I invented only one of them! I won't indicate which one that is, lest I offend someone who may have also invented it independently. The rest of these drills I have picked up here and there over the past 45 years. I have identified the creator of each drill for which I have that information—which, unfortunately, is only a few of them.

2
Single Mark Concepts
and
Preliminary Drills

CONCEPTS

What is a "Single Mark"?

A single marked retrieve (a.k.a. "single mark" or more simply "single") is a marked retrieve involving the fall of only one bird. A "marked retrieve" is one in which the dog sees the bird fall, as opposed to a "blind retrieve," in which he doesn't. In a marked retrieve, the dog is expected to identify ("mark") and remember the location the fall, so that, when sent, he can run directly to the "area of the fall" and hunt within that area until he finds the bird.

The "Area of the Fall"

The "area of the fall" is the area around a fallen bird in which the dog may legitimately hunt, that is, hunt without "disturbing too much cover." No retriever can mark so well that he "pins," "steps on," or "buttons" every bird, that is, runs or swims out directly to it. Terrain variations, cover changes, wind conditions, and scenting conditions often make that impossible. So the best we can expect, at least on challenging

Opposite: The author and his Golden, Mickey, swim back to the line (many years ago) after the non-correction for blinking a duck, which is discussed in the text. Not only did this incident create a long-term problem, but it also elicited only minimal obedience to the "Fetch!" command. Notice that Mickey is dragging the duck by its bill, with the rest of the bird floating along beside him. (On the positive side, neither dog nor handler is "cheating," that is, returning by the nearby land.) Photo by Theresa Spencer.

marks, is that the dog will hunt a reasonably small area around the bird until he finds it. That reasonably small area is called "the area of the fall." We don't fault a dog for hunting within it. In fact, experienced retriever people enjoy watching a dog hunt the area of a fall crisply and cleanly. However, if a retriever hunts outside of the area of the fall, he disturbs cover unnecessarily and thereby risks flushing birds out of gun range.

The size of the area of the fall for any given mark is a matter of judgment. Over many decades, retriever folks have developed the following as an initial rough estimate: The area of the fall is a circle around the bird with a radius measuring about 10% (or a diameter about 20%) of the distance from the "line" to the bird, the "line" being the spot from which the dog saw the bird fall. Circumstances can affect the size, shape, and even the location of the area of the fall. For example, in a double mark, the area of the fall for the second bird retrieved (the "memory bird") is larger than that for the first bird retrieved (the "go-bird"), because the dog must remember the former while retrieving the latter. A strong wind not only changes the shape of the area from circular to conical, but also shifts it downwind so the bird lies nearer the narrow end of the cone. Retrieverites make these adjustments to be reasonable in their expectations of their dogs. But, no matter how it is defined for a particular mark, the area of the fall sets the boundaries within which the dog should hunt for the bird. As long as he is hunting diligently within that area, he's doing a good job, even if he hunts quite some time before producing the bird.

A "Loose Hunt"

In dog-games (field trials, hunt tests, and working certificate tests) the judges fault a dog that hunts outside the area of the fall for any significant time for having a "loose hunt." The longer and looser the hunt, the more serious the fault. The handler of such a dog must use his own judgment to determine when he should "handle" him to the bird (with whistle and arm signals *a la* blind retrieve). "Handling on a mark" also constitutes a fault and, barring unusual circumstances, a serious one. Thus the handler must decide when his dog will be penalized more for continuing a loose hunt than he would be for handling on a mark. The general rule is to play it safe and handle too soon rather than too late, for a long and loose hunt leaves a worse impression on judges than a quick and clean "handle."

In actual hunting, each person must determine how much of a loose hunt he will tolerate. My observations indicate that most hunters are less patient than even the strictest dog-game judges. In fact, many hunters, in their anxiety to collect every bird shot, begin to handle their dogs while they are still hunting well within the area of the fall. Some, quite foolishly, begin handling before the dog reaches the area of the fall! Nothing could damage a dog's marking ability more.

Dealing with "Loose Hunts" in Training

How should you deal with those situations in training when your dog cannot find a mark? If he already "handles," that is, takes arm and whistle signals, you may be tempted to remain at the line and handle him to any mark he can't find. Generally speaking, that is a bad idea. If you regularly help him find marks this way, he will begin to expect it whenever he has the least difficulty finding a fall. He will "pop" (stop and sit facing you, expecting an arm signal) just as if you had blown the *Sit*-whistle. If you oblige him regularly, his marking will atrophy.

Instead of handling him, you may be tempted to run out and help him find the dummy yourself. Unless absolutely necessary, this is also a bad idea. When you have to do this (for example, when using a dummy launcher), you should do it in a clearly "unfriendly" way, to convince your dog that you are greatly displeased with him, in fact, that he is in big trouble until he gets the dummy in his mouth. Otherwise, he will come to look forward to your assistance—so much so that he won't persevere in hunting for marks.

I learned the folly of "friendly" assistance years ago with a young Golden named Mickey that I was running in Derby stakes. In a water series at the local retriever club's monthly fun trial, he "blinked" (shied away from) a quacking, hissing mallard. From the line, I commanded *Fetch!*, but Mickey refused to grab the threatening bird. So I dove in and swam out there. The club had a rule against disciplining dogs in these fun trials, lest newcomers in the gallery be shocked. So, when I reached the scene of the crime, I commanded *Fetch!* very gently. Mickey grabbed the duck and we swam back to the line together. Although, of course, we were eliminated from that trial, I felt very good about the whole incident. I had made my point (or so I thought), and had done it so gently that the most sensitive soul in the gallery could not have complained.

In the following month's fun trial, in the first water series, Mickey jumped into the water and popped, apparently waiting for me to jump in and join him! Since I had done this so graciously in that previous trial, he figured I wanted to swim out with him regularly, at least in trials. But he wouldn't do this in training. We blew three trials this way. Eventually, in a training session, I set up a simulated trial (cars, people, noise, and so forth). Predictably, he jumped in the water and popped. When he turn around, he saw me almost flying through the air at him, screaming as I came. In short, I landed all over him, physically and verbally. He never popped like that again, in training or in trials. He won the Derby stake in the next fun trial, which was the last one of the year. But I paid a price for those three trials he messed up. In the club's little Derby Dog of the Year competition, he had been way ahead. But those three trials allowed another dog to pass him. We lost that trophy by one-half point!

Never again have I been gentle when I've had to go out to help a dog find a mark. Instead, I let him know I'm mightily upset, that he can redeem himself only by getting the dummy in his mouth. That way, the dog learns to hunt on his own rather than seek my company. (Should you find it absolutely necessary to go out and help your dog find a mark, by all means, "Go therefore and do thou in like manner.")

If, in training, you shouldn't handle your dog to marks he can't find and you shouldn't go out to help him personally, how should you deal with such situations? Ideally, the thrower should help your dog (on your signal, of course). For reasons I don't fully understand, this doesn't incline the dog to give up easily and look for help. But the thrower should help your dog in a very precise manner. He should walk toward the dummy while hollering "Hey! Hey! Hey!" (or blowing a duck call) to attract your dog's attention. If your dog returns to the area of the fall, the thrower should give him a chance to find the dummy without further help. If he still can't find it, the thrower should walk to the dummy, pick it up, step back a couple of steps, attract your dog's attention, *then toss the dummy straight up so it again lands exactly where it was before.* Your dog will run in and pick it up and bring it to you. Then, you should rerun the test, so your dog can see the fall from the line again knowing precisely where the dummy is landing. Such reruns improve your dog's marking significantly.

If, when helping your dog out, the thrower were to toss the dummy somewhere other than where it landed on the initial run, he would destroy the value of rerunning the test. On the rerun, your dog will mark the fall as landing precisely where he found it the first time. If, because of improper "help" from the thrower, he found it in the wrong place, he will mismark the fall on the rerun, thinking it is coming down where he found it the previous time. He will go to that spot, find nothing, and become confused. (Make sure your throwers understand all this before you set up a test.)

When should you signal for help from the thrower? As long as your dog is hunting diligently in the area of the fall, let him hunt. But if he slacks off or wanders off—and especially if he heads back toward you—signal for the thrower to help him.

Line Manners

"Line manners" is a dog-game term, referring primarily to the dog's manners at the "line," or starting position for a test (or "series"). Since the handler's deportment affects the dog's behavior, the handler's

Good basic line manners for a single mark. Handler Mary Jo Gallagher and her Flat-Coated Retriever, "Fortune" (CH. Windfall's Flatland Fortune SH CDX NA WCX), are set up properly. Fortune is looking in the direction of the mark and Mary Jo is looking at Fortune.

manners at the line are also important. In dog-games, the term "line manners" includes everything both the dog and handler do while at the line and under judgment.

Line Manners in Dog-Games

For the dog, proper line manners for a single mark are quite simple. He should heel (typically on lead) to the line, and sit quietly wherever his handler sets him up. As the bird goes up and comes down, he should remain reasonably steady, even though his handler may legally restrain him. When sent to retrieve, the dog should leave with enthusiasm. When he returns with the bird, he need not sit at heel to deliver (although that is preferred), but he should hold the bird until told to release it, and he should surrender it willingly on command. Then he should heel tractably away from the line.

For the handler, proper line manners for single marks are also quite simple. He should heel his dog to the line promptly after being called by the judges or marshal. At the line, he should take whatever position the judges indicate, and set his dog up to see the fall. Then he should indicate to the judges—usually with a slight movement of his hand behind his back—that he is ready. The judges then signal to the "guns" (two or three people stationed together out in the field to throw and shoot birds). Since, in hunting tests, the "guns" are normally hidden, one of them either fires a blank pistol or blows a duck or pheasant call to attract the dog's attention. Then one of them throws the bird. If the bird is a "flier" (a live bird), two guns shoot it so it falls approximately where the judges want it. If it's a "control bird" (a thrown dead bird), one of the guns "pops" (fires a blank shell) when the bird is near the top of its arc. After the bird is down, one of the judges tells the handler he may send his dog to retrieve. During all this time, that is, from the time the handler indicates he is ready until the judge tells him to send his dog (by calling the dog's number), the handler should remain quiet and motionless. After the judge calls his number, the handler may send his dog to retrieve. When his dog returns with the bird, he should take it smoothly, without touching or otherwise intimidating his dog.

You will encounter single marks in the lowest level of hunt tests and in working certificate tests. In either, as a handler, your only job is to facilitate and simplify your dog's work. The judges should see mostly your dog. You should be almost transparent. If, while in the gallery, you notice that some handler has captivating grace and style at the line—poetry in motion, every move a picture, every sound a concert, and so forth—you're watching a performer, not a handler. Enjoy the show if you like, but don't imitate it. Keep your own handling simple and unobtrusive. Your dog will work better, and score better.

In a single mark test, your job is quite simple. Heel your dog to the line, have him sit beside you so he is facing the area in which the bird will fall. Since you are allowed to control your dog with a lead or belt cord, by all means do so, no matter how steady he may be. Disdaining such aids is show-boating, for which you get no extra points—but your dog will be dropped (disqualified) if he breaks.

You may send your dog anytime after the judge calls your number. Please note: You don't have to send him immediately. Make sure he is locked in on the fall before you launch him. If, for example, your dog glances away from the fall, bring his attention back to it before you send him. In sending him, should you give him both a verbal command and a hand signal? Many do, but (methinks) more from tradition than rational thought. Look at it from your dog's viewpoint. He has just watched a bird fall, and he's aching to be on his way to retrieve it. He is staring holes in the place where it fell. Then suddenly the boss's big mitt penetrates his peripheral vision—or worse, blocks his view—distracting him from the fall. How can this help the dog? Whenever your dog is locked in tightly on a mark, you'll help him more if you send him with just a verbal command (normally his call name), without a hand signal.

One exception does apply: If your dog is a chronic breaker, you may be able to keep him steady, or at least somewhat steadier, by consistently preceding the vocal command with a hand signal. Chronic breakers usually mark very well, so they can tolerate such distractions better than less talented markers. To be effective, the hand signal should *not* release the breaker. It's just a preliminary signal, a cue that tells him you are about to release him with the verbal. Thus, to make the hand signal effective, you should put your hand down, then wait one to three seconds before giving the verbal command. Use a steady hand. Simply place it beside his head; don't wave it around; above all, don't flick it forward. Moving your hand after it enters his peripheral vision tempts him to break.

So much for basic single mark handling at the line. In some hunting tests, the judges may complicate your life by requiring that you sit on a stool, or in a blind, or even in a boat. You may even have to hold a shotgun. If so, follow their instructions as precisely as possible.

However, before indicating that you are ready, make sure your dog is sitting so he faces the area of the anticipated fall.

Line Manners in Hunting

In actual hunting, you will have to vary this handling procedure. In duck hunting, for example, you certainly can't stand out in the open with your dog sitting at heel beside you. Both you and your dog may be inside the blind until you knock down some birds. Or perhaps your dog will be beside your blind. Even so, in training, use the basic setup (you standing, with your dog sitting at heel beside you) most of the time. In fact, use it regularly, except when introducing your dog to various hunting or hunting test paraphernalia (stool, blinds, boats, and so forth). In normal training, you can deal more effectively with whatever problems you may encounter if you are standing on *terra firma* and your dog is sitting at heel beside you. When you are accustoming him to stools, blinds, boats, and so forth, simplify the tests. Make them so easy that your dog can ho-hum them. That way, during those special training sessions, you and your dog will have to deal with only the hunting equipment problem. Similarly, introduce your retriever to whatever special equipment you use in actual hunting—blinds, boats, whatever—in special training sessions, with very simple marks.

Bare Ground

Throughout this book, you will see the term "bare ground." It includes not only bare ground as such, but also any field or area in which the vegetation doesn't prevent your dog, while still at the line, from seeing the dummy he is to retrieve lying on the ground. Thus, "bare ground" can be a beautifully manicured lawn. It can be a fairway of an unused golf course. It can be a well-used park with scattered patches of short grass. It can be a school yard covered with sand and gravel. Or it can, of course, be ground that is truly bare. For certain drills, your dog should be able to see the dummies from the line. For these I specify "bare ground," meaning any area in which your dog can see the dummy from the line.

PRELIMINARY DRILLS

Before getting into the actual single-mark training drills, we should go through a number of peripheral drills, techniques, and procedures that bear directly or indirectly on single marks. Among them, the following are covered in the rest of this chapter: steadying; honoring; drills to introduce various pieces of training and hunting equipment, such as throwers, birds, gunfire, boats, and decoys. (Appendix I describes all the equipment used in retriever training and Appendix II explains how to introduce your retriever to the electronic collar.) The next chapter, Chapter 3, covers drills for dealing with various mouth problems that may crop up anytime in training a retriever.

Steadying

A steady retriever sits beside his handler until sent to retrieve. While the bird is going up and coming down, he doesn't break or even creep forward. He just sits there, staring, first, at the bird while it's in the air, and then at the place where it has fallen. He may be quivering to go, but he remains sitting. Anything less than that—breaks, "controlled" breaks, or even creeping—is a form of unsteadiness that needs to be dealt with in training.

You should steady your dog through a separate process on bare ground, not as part of his normal work on single marks in cover. If you steady your dog while working in cover, he will frequently fail to find the mark because of the hassle associated with steadying. Enough of such failures will damage his confidence in his marking ability. He may even "no-go" (refuse to leave your side when sent). That problem is more easily avoided than cured, especially in a youngster still doing only single marks. To avoid that disaster, you should steady your dog on bare ground with highly visible white dummies, which he can see from the line, or from anywhere else in the area. That way, he will never fail to complete a retrieve, no matter how much of a hassle you have while keeping him steady at the line.

Start out with relatively short retrieves (20 to 30 yards), so you can repeat them several times without tiring your dog. Heel him to the line and put the belt cord on him. You want to teach him to sit there until you send him. Thus, your command to retrieve (typically his call name), must take on a magic quality. It, and it alone, must release him. The belt cord, properly used, will gradually give it that magic. To use the belt cord properly, you must keep it loose, so your dog can't feel it— until he breaks. Then it magically snubs him up and won't let him go. However, when you say his name, he can take off and run freely off the belt cord without feeling it. If you keep the belt cord so tight he can feel

Proper use of the belt cord for steadying. Marilyn Corbin has her Golden Retriever, "Summer" (Benden's Up With The Sun JH, CGC, WC), on a loose belt cord. As long as Summer remains steady, she won't feel any pressure from the cord, but if she attempts to break, it will bring her up short.

the pressure, you "telegraph your punch" and destroy the belt cord's effectiveness.

Set your dog up at the line, install the *loose* belt cord, and signal for a throw. As the dummy rises, your dog will lunge forward, just as he has been doing all along. But this time, you jerk him back and make him sit again. Actually, it seldom goes that smoothly. In my own case at least, the dog usually bucks and spins until we're both on the ground with the belt cord wrapped around sundry body parts (human and canine). No matter. He hasn't escaped and the dummy is in plain sight. I regain my vertical stance, make the dog sit beside me, and send him. He runs out, picks up the dummy, and returns. I repeat this several times, as long as he remains fresh and enthusiastic. Usually by the end of the first session, the dog is beginning to catch on and I'm beginning to regain some of my lost dignity. No more going to the mat. The dog still lunges forward, but with less determination. After a few session, he acts as if he understands what I want. In fact, he does, but he hasn't yet figured out just how serious I am about it. He continues to break at least now and then.

Thus, I keep the belt cord on him for a long time, even after we move into cover—30 to 90 days, depending on how strong-willed he is.

With most dogs, that is enough. Thereafter, if the dog breaks, you need only holler, "No! Heel!" to bring the beast back. However, my Chessy, Beaver, was, to say the very least, not "like most dogs." When it was time to take him off the belt cord, I somehow knew he would test me as soon as possible, and that hollering at him wouldn't accomplish anything. So, when I removed the belt cord, I started going to the line carrying heavy artillery—a long and heavy leather whip. (It looks worse than it is, for it's quite thick. The thin ones inflict the most pain.) Before calling for the birds, I always slung that whip over my shoulder, with the grip in my right hand.

Sure enough, Beaver broke one evening, and I was ready for him. Hollering "No! Heel!" loud enough to be heard in the next county, I stepped forward and brought that whip down on his departing rump with all the force I could put into it. He got it all! But he didn't stop. He didn't even slow down. He didn't yelp. He didn't so much as glance back at me. He gave no indication that he noticed that stroke with the whip as he raced out, picked up the bird, and strutted back. In delivering, he looked up at me, seeming to say, "So, genius, whatcha gonna do now?"

Frankly, I was baffled. I went back to the belt cord for a while, but he didn't even try to break then. When I took it off again, I knew this crafty beast would break, and I wouldn't be able to do a thing about it.

The infamous "Beaver" (Rumrunner's Redlion Beaver JH).

But, strange as it may seem, he never broke again! Never in his entire life! As near as I can figure out from whatever little I know about Chesapeake psychology, here's what happened: Contrary to appearances, Beaver really felt that shot with the whip; but he figured he'd already paid the price, so he may as well get the bird; however, he decided he would never, ever, ever pay that price again. Such reactions make Chesapeakes fascinating critters.

Honoring

A dog "honors" the work of another dog when he sits quietly at heel while the other dog marks and retrieves one or more birds. In a typical dog-game honoring test, both dogs are at the line, but separated by a few yards. Both dogs watch the falls. But only the "working dog" retrieves them. The "honoring dog" must remain sitting at heel until the judges release him, after which his handler heels him off the line. In field trials and most working certificate tests, the honoring dog must sit. However, in hunt tests, the handler may have his dog either sit or lie down. The latter is the more "secure" position. Also, sometimes in hunt tests, the dog must honor some distance from his handler.

Hunt tests, field trials, and working certificate tests don't require honoring until the dog reaches those levels and stakes that require multiple marks. Thus, you could delay this training until then (in *Training Retrievers for the Marshes and Meadows*, I placed it in the chapter on double marks for precisely that reason). However, those working in training groups of at least three people can introduce honoring in single marks, simultaneously with steadying, and to great advantage.

Do this work on bare ground, with white dummies, for visibility. Put your thrower 20 to 30 yards out. At the line, establish two "positions," one for each dog involved in this drill. Both handlers should have their dogs on belt cords, and both should realize how devastating noisy handling by either of them can be to the other person's dog. For example, let's say the working dog has just been sent, and the honoring dog tries to break. If the honoring dog's handler screams "NO! HEEL! GET BACK HERE, YOU WORTHLESS—!" and so on, the working dog will almost certainly think the yelling is directed at him. This is especially true of young dogs, which is what we are dealing with here. The working dog may turn and slink back to his owner. He may just lie down and tremble. At the very least, he will glance around at the other handler and his dog—when he should be focused on the dummy. Similarly, if the honoring dog remains where he belongs, but the working dog breaks, excess noise by the working dog handler could confuse the honoring dog. Is he being yelled at for sitting there? Clearly, whether you are handling the working or the honoring dog, *you should make your corrections with your belt cord, not your vocal chords*. Say nothing. Just jerk your dog back roughly to where he belongs with your belt cord.

In combining steadying and honoring, you and your training buddy can take turns working and honoring. But before each throw, decide which dog is the working dog, lest you send both dogs at the same time, and create a canine turf wars over the dummy. With both dogs on loose belt cords, the working dog handler should first ask the other handler if he's ready. If he is, then the working dog handler should signal for a throw. When he sends his dog, he should do it quietly; the dog is right

Using belt cords for honoring. Mary Jo Gallagher and Fortune are working while Marilyn Corbin and Summer are honoring. Mary Jo has just sent Fortune and he is running off of the released belt cord. Summer is attempting to break, but Marilyn is restraining her with her belt cord, not with her vocal chords (which would disturb the working dog).

next him, so he needn't shout his command to retrieve. The honoring dog handler should control his dog with the belt cord, without a sound. When the working dog returns with the dummy, the two dog/handler teams should switch roles. But, to speed things up, they should not switch places.

Nota bene: To help your dog understand the difference between being steady and honoring, give the *Stay* command only when he is honoring. It will come to mean, "Relax, Dude, you ain't goin' no-place no-how this time." When yours is the working dog, say nothing to steady him (other than *Sit*, or the *Sit*-whistle when you arrive at the line). After all, you are using the belt cord to teach him *not* to go until he hears your command to retrieve. You don't need a special steadying word. Let *Stay* mean he will not be allowed to retrieve this time, and it will serve you well in honoring. If you use it also when he will retrieve, you turn it into meaningless noise to him.

Drills to Introduce Equipment

Throwers

A "thrower" is a person who throws dummies or birds for your dog to retrieve. (In tests and trials, such persons are given the more dignified name of "guns," but in training sessions, they are just lowly "throwers." In training groups, each person takes his turn acting as a thrower for the other folks in the group.) Why do we need someone else to throw for us? Because none of us can throw a dummy far enough to turn it into a significant single mark. So, we have one of our training buddies carry some dummies out beyond our throwing range—usually well beyond it—and toss them for us.

However, having someone else throw will probably confuse your dog initially. He may well try to deliver to your buddy instead of you. Look at it from your dog's point of view: When you threw the dummy, he had to take it to you; so when someone else throws it, why shouldn't he take it to that person? Not all dogs make this mistake, of course, but enough of them do to justify talking about it here.

The easiest way to solve this problem is to prevent it. When you introduce a thrower, put him where your youngster can't get to him. I do this by putting the thrower in a neighboring backyard, with a

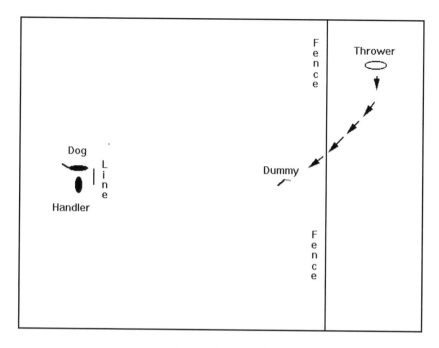

Figure 1. Introducing a Thrower.

chainlink fence between him and us. From there he throws the dummy over the fence into my yard. After picking it up, the dog is blocked (by the fence) from going to the thrower. I, of course, loudly encourage the dog to come to me, and make a big fuss over him when he does. When out in the field, I have had the thrower stand in the bed of a pickup truck, where my dog couldn't reach him. With real hard cases—dogs that persisted in trying to get to these inaccessible throwers—I have gone to the retractable lead, so I could pull the determined little beastie back to me.

Birds

Like most, I introduce puppies to dead pigeons very early (5 to 10 weeks of age). However, I do it in a non-stressful manner, lest the pup develop a fear of feathers. After stuffing a dead (but not frozen) pigeon in my vest, I take the pup for a romp in a field with light to moderate cover. We amble around here and there. When he is distracted by something, I drop the pigeon in cover and keep walking.

Then the pup and I gradually wander around to the downwind of the bird. He scents it, and may do any of several things:

- He may lie down and start to eat it. (*"Hmmm,"* I think, *"an 800-pound gorilla! Little guy, give me that bird! Your jaws are strong, but at this age, I can still pry them open. There. Next time, you'll get a frozen pigeon, and you'll be on a retractable lead!"*)

- He may race in, grab it, and run off. (*"Hmmm, an aggressive little rascal. Next time you'll get a frozen pigeon and a retractable lead."*)

- He may pick it up and look at me. (*"Hey, kid, I like your style! Here, puppy; here, puppy; oh, nice puppy; let me hold your collar and pet you while you hold this new treasure. You can keep it until you drop it. There. Let's walk some more and do it again."*)

- He may sniff it, but refuse to pick it up. (*I say nothing, do nothing, until he abandons it. Then I pick it up, walk awhile again, and drop it somewhere else.*)

- He may ignore it. (*I worry about either his nose or his birdiness, but I don't give up until he has reacted like this through several successive sessions, with several drops per session.*)

After working through this routine until the pup brings me the pigeon consistently and without the retractable lead—which may take several sessions—I start using pigeons (frozen or unfrozen, depending on his reactions) in regular training.

Later on, with larger birds like ducks and pheasants, I use the same routine. Perhaps because of my background with Goldens, I worry about each new species of bird intimidating the dog. So I let the dog stumble onto the first one, in fact the first several. If he balks at a specific bird, say a duck, I repeat the drill with a "lighter" duck. I de-gut the bird, remove the head, wings, and legs, so the dog has to deal with just the torso, which is small and light enough for any normal-sized retriever.

One final comment—a warning, really: Never introduce a new species of bird through the force-breaking command *Fetch*. So many people permanently intimidate their dogs this way, especially with ducks. Remember: We do *not* force-break retrievers to get them to retrieve; we do it to get reliable delivery to hand, especially in water work, and to set up a basis for curing various mouth problems. If your dog won't retrieve ducks naturally, he won't do it through force-breaking either. And, if you introduce a new species of bird through force-breaking, you run a major risk of so intimidating your dog that he will never retrieve that species naturally. Why risk it?

Gun-Proofing

Retrievers are quite stable in temperament, at least when compared to pointing dogs. Over the centuries breeders of these latter have developed dogs that are "tightly wound," nervous dogs that cover lots of ground as quickly as possible to find birds in the uplands. Being thusly wired, pointing dogs are highly susceptible to gun-shyness. Most of the drills—as well as the superstitions, old wives' tales, and other non-sense—for gun-proofing a dog originated in the world of pointing dogs.

Over the centuries, retriever breeders have developed laid-back dogs, calm dogs that will sit beside the blind for hours between retrieves. (Granted, most retrievers abound with energy. But they aren't jumpy and flighty the way so many pointing dogs are.) Thus, retrievers are not highly susceptible to gun-shyness. In fact, gun-proofing a retriever requires no special drills, just a little common sense.

After you have introduced your pup to throwers and lengthened his retrieves to about 100 yards on bare ground, you can gun-proof him easily. Up until this time, your thrower has hollered "Hey! Hey! Hey!" to get your pup's attention before tossing each dummy. That "Hey! Hey! Hey!" has become music to your youngster's ears, because it always precedes a retrieve. To gun-proof him, you only need transfer the warm feeling he has for "Hey! Hey! Hey!" to the sound of a gun. Once you have done that, he will love the gun.

Start out with your thrower out about 100 yards. He should holler the usual "Hey! Hey! Hey!" before he throws, but then as he throws, he should also shoot a blank pistol. At 100 yards, your pup will hardly notice the little "pop" from the gun. After a few repetitions, all at 100 yards, your thrower should stop hollering "Hey! Hey! Hey!" and just fire the pistol. The rest is obvious. Gradually shorten the distance between the line and your thrower. If, at some distance, your dog reacts negatively— which I can't imagine if you proceed gradually—go back to longer retrieves for a while.

When you move into cover, use the blank pistol for all his retrieves. Your youngster will love that sound. Later, after you are absolutely sure of his abiding affection for the sound of a blank pistol, introduce the shotgun. Start with a 20-gauge at 100 yards, and gradually shorten the distance, as his reaction indicates. Then bring out the big 12-gauge and go back to 100 yards.

So much for how to do it. Perhaps, for your own protection, I should mention a couple of popular ways *not* to do it. Do not take a puppy out and "test him to see if he's gun-shy" (by firing a 12-gauge near him with no preliminary work). Do that with 100 puppies and at least 95 of them would be "gun-shy," the other five would have been born deaf. Do not take a puppy to a skeet, trap, or sporting clays range "to accustom him to the sound of guns." Such a series of startling, unexpected, and unpredictable explosions would make a brass monkey gun-shy.

Duck and Pheasant Calls

If you have hunt-test ambitions, you should also introduce your dog to the sound of duck and pheasant calls. In hunt tests, these are often used by hidden guns to attract the dog's attention before they throw the bird. To introduce your dog to these cue sounds, have your thrower blow the call instead of hollering "Hey! Hey! Hey!" After your dog is adequately gun-proofed, have your thrower blow the call before the throw and shoot the blank pistol while the dummy or bird is in the air. That is a common sequence of events in hunt tests. (Sometimes the hidden guns fire a blank before throwing and then again as the bird is in the air, so do it that way, too.)

Incidentally, if your thrower is less than a talented duck and pheasant caller, don't worry about it. Let him make whatever sound he can with the calls. I've heard some pretty awful noise coming out of calls in hunt tests.

Boats

If you plan to hunt from a boat, or run hunt tests (in which the line is sometimes in a boat), you should prepare your dog long before the occasion arises. You can do this most easily if you start out on land. For this, I have an old johnboat in the backyard. If you don't have one, you should still introduce your dog to boats on land. Pull the boat up on shore. This allows your dog to become used to the contraption itself before he has to develop sea-legs to deal with its instability when floating.

First, let him investigate the boat on his own. Let him walk around it, sniff it, and so on. Next, climb aboard yourself and encourage him to join you. Don't force him. Just coax him near you. When he reaches the side of the boat, pet and praise him. When he comes in to join you, continue to pet and praise him. Do nothing else until he seems quite relaxed in the boat. That may take more than one session. Next, with him in the boat with you, toss a dummy out on land and send him to retrieve it. When he delivers to you in the boat, make a big fuss over him. Repeat this until he is quite comfortable retrieving from the boat on land. As a final step on land, stand some distance from the boat, with your dog sitting at heel, and toss the dummy into the boat and have him retrieve it.

Next, take him for a ride on the water. Row around and let him get used to the instability of the craft. Don't ask him to retrieve until he seems to have his sea-legs, that is, until he's comfortable enough to walk around in the floating boat. Then partially beach the boat, so it is reasonably but not completely stable. Toss a dummy into the water and send him to retrieve it. He will get a little rocking sensation as he leaves the boat. When he can handle that, put out a little ways, still in shallow water, toss the dummy in the water again, and send him. At this stage, when he returns, start taking the dummy before he re-enters the boat. This will be essential later in deep water, where, if he were to carry a bird while struggling to climb aboard, he would mash it. Continue this process until he has no problem either jumping from or climbing in the boat in deep water. To help him re-board, after you take the dummy, lift his front feet up onto the side of the boat, then hold the back of his head firmly to give him leverage for pulling himself in.

Decoys

As with boats, you should begin to introduce your youngster to decoys on land, where you can correct him more easily. In the backyard, put out a spread of several decoys. Put your dog on lead and heel him around through the blocks. Whenever he tries to investigate one, jerk the lead, say "No!" and continue heeling. Continue this until he ignores them completely.

Next, with the same decoy spread laid out, stand near them and toss a dummy off to the side. Send your dog to retrieve it. If he pesters the decoys either going or coming, holler "No!" Then go back a step (to heeling through the decoys) for a while before again tossing a dummy off to the side. When the dog consistently retrieves from off to the side with-

Marilyn is heeling Summer through a spread of decoys on land. As Summer attempts to investigate one, Marilyn snaps the lead and says "No! Heel!"

After the correction shown in the previous picture, Summer resumes heeling properly, ignoring the decoy.

out incident, toss the dummy straight over and beyond the decoys and send him. If he yields to temptation, correct him as above and go back a step (to tossing the dummy off to the side) for a while. When he ignores the decoys while retrieving a dummy tossed straight beyond them, toss it so it falls right in the middle of the decoys and send him. When he ignores the decoys on such a retrieve, he's ready to advance to water.

Put several decoys in shallow water. Stand on shore and repeat the above drill, first tossing the dummy down the shore, then out to sea beyond the decoys, and finally right in the middle of them. Corrections in water are not so easily administered, so don't rush into any part of this work before your dog is ready.

After this initial decoy-proofing, remember to use decoys in your normal training sessions quite often. Too many people forget this, and their dogs begin to backslide from lack of exposure. You should even put decoys out in some of your land tests—especially large goose decoys.

3
Drills for Mouth Problems

Before studying drills designed specifically for single marks, you should learn about drills and other training techniques for curing the various mouth problems that may crop up at any time with any dog: hardmouth, stickiness, sloppy-mouth, poor delivery, and vocalizing. As you will see, curing most of these problems requires that the dog be force-broken. If that term causes you some concern, then you have probably been exposed only to what I call "Hell Week" force-breaking. Hell Week is popular, at least among ill-informed retriever trainers. As the name suggests, Hell Week doesn't take long, but it is extremely rough, so rough in fact that I wouldn't use it even if it were the only technique available. Fortunately, it isn't. I have long used, and advocated, the slow and gentle "Sanborn" technique, which birddog trainer David Sanborn developed back in the 1880s. You can find this technique explained fully in my book, *Training Retrievers for the Marshes and Meadows.*

HARDMOUTH

Definition

"Hardmouth" means different things to different people. Some suffer the vapors over a few mussed feathers. Others overlook any amount of damage as long as the dog doesn't totally consume birds. Most fall between those extremes, requiring that the delivered bird be fit for human consumption, but not faulting purely cosmetic damage.

Going along with that majority, *let's define hardmouth as any mouthing by the dog that leaves a bird unfit for the table.*

Causes

Heredity

Some dogs have genes that inclines them to hardmouth. In fact, some breeds seem to carry these genes more than others. Several pointing breeds produce a high incidence of hardmouth—perhaps because of the hounds in their ancestry. For example, my Shorthair-in-residence, Erick, seems to have been born with the retrieving instincts of an 800-pound gorilla, for initially he ate birds where they fell. Of course, as soon as I realized he had this problem, I restricted his retrieving to dummies until I was in position to cure him. More on that later.

Accident

A freak accident can turn a gentle-mouthed dog into a bird-flattener. Back in the mid-1950s, my Weimaraner, Misty, was soft-mouthed to a fault. In water, she didn't even grip a bird or dummy. She simply pushed it along ahead of her with her open mouth. One July afternoon, I shot a pigeon over water for her. She swam out, and started pushing the bird back toward me. Just before she reached shore, the bird came to life and tried to fly away. Misty leapt high out of the water after it. She caught it, but in doing so, she accidentally flattened it. When she delivered it to me, it looked like it had lost a territorial dispute with an 18-wheeler.

Had I ignored that accident, she would have had another, more deliberate "accident" very soon, maybe even on the next bird. And another and another and so on until she would have become incorrigible. Realizing that, I applied the cure for that type of hardmouth immediately. More on that later.

Bad Birds

Many, perhaps most, hardmouthed dogs start down that road because of a severely shot-up or otherwise damaged bird. This can happen while hunting, if you shoot a bird too close to the gun. More often, at least for retrievers, it happens in training or in dog-games, when a thrower re-uses a dead bird he should have discarded. Examples of bad birds: soggy dead pigeons and upland gamebirds used over and over for water retrieves; dead hen pheasants carrying eggs, which break and leak out when the thrown bird hits the ground; any dead bird, wet or dry, with skin torn or intestines exposed.

Anyone who uses a dead pigeon or upland gamebird more than once for water work invites hardmouth. Unlike ducks, these are delicate birds. Their (non-waterproof) feathers fall out easily when soaked. Their thin skins split at a touch, especially in water. With the feathers gone and the skin split, such a bird presents the dog with an irresistible taste of fresh meat. Munch, munch, munch.

I learned this back in the early 1970s when judging the amateur stake at a nearby retriever fun trial. After the first three series, one dog was so far ahead of the competition that we only ran the water blind as a formality. We gave the bird planter a sack of wet dead pigeons from the previous series. Our "clear winner" lined the blind. Another great series, I thought, what a dog! But, on the way back, he ate the bird—every ounce of meat, and every bone—leaving only a trail of feathers on the water behind him. The stunned owner told me the dog had never before damaged a bird. I didn't believe him then, but I do now.

Only later, after talking with other retriever folks, did I come to understand the problem. Since no other dog damaged a bird in that series, I had blamed the dog. Wrong, wrong, wrong. That is the insidious part of re-using pigeons and upland birds in water. It doesn't create a problem with every dog every time, but it does so with enough regularity to make it a very, very foolish practice. If you must re-use dead birds in water, stick with ducks. You may safely re-use them as long they remain intact, fully feathered, and floating high. If you lack dead ducks, use dummies for water training.

Even on land, do not re-use *any* dead bird (pigeon, upland bird, or duck) unless it is in good condition. My Chessy, Beaver, ate a pigeon in a land series at an AKC hunting test because the inexperienced throwers gave him a bedraggled bird with intestines hanging out. They apologized later, but I still had to put Beaver through the cure.

Bad Dummies

Old canvas dummies with rotting covers, especially when the insides are leaking out, can create hardmouth. I have seen several normally soft-mouthed dogs chew such dummies like kids chew bubble gum. Why? Beats me. I'm just telling you what I've seen.

Even plastic knobby dummies are not problem-free. For example, my

Golden, Brandy, rolled the small ones in his mouth. That is an early warning sign of impending hardmouth. I switched him to large plastic knobbies, which he didn't—probably couldn't—roll. Another example: In lining drills, Beaver brought in small plastic dummies from the dummy piles in "flocks" of two or three. That can create all sorts of problems, hardmouth included. To avoid yet another battle of wills with him, I switched to large dummies, for which he had the cargo capacity for just one.

Not Enough Birds in Training

If you train with birds infrequently, every bird will be a *big deal* to your dog. Therefore, every bird will bring out any latent hardmouth tendencies he may have. Years ago, I noticed that my Golden, Brandy, was quite rough with birds whenever we used them in training. He wasn't really hardmouthed, just rough. I talked to pro D. L. Walters about this. He asked me if I used birds in training very often. I told him I didn't. He told me to give Brandy birds as often as possible, in fact, to make birds old hat for him. I did and the problem went away. I don't know whether Brandy would have become hardmouthed had I continued using birds infrequently, but it was certainly a strong possibility. So giving your dog plenty of birds in training could prevent this problem from coming up. An ounce of prevention . . . .

Trainer Error

Finally, a trainer can cause hardmouth in any number of non-intelligent ways. Like playing tug-o-war with his dog, especially with a bird. At delivery, the dog should release his hold on the bird at the trainer's command, and then back off. If he doesn't, the boss should 'splain it so's the beast can understand it, normally by applying his knee vigorously to the dog's chest. A handler should *never* pull the bird away from the dog.

Another trainer error: teasing the dog with a bird, such as by dangling it just out of reach to induce the dog to jump at it. If the dog actually grabs it, a game of tug-o-war almost certainly follows.

Yet another one: Leaving the dog unattended with a dead bird, like behind the blind or in the back of a station wagon or pickup truck. Left alone long enough, he will eat the bird, no matter how well-mannered he is.

I could go on with this litany of trainer errors that cause hardmouth, but those already mentioned are sufficiently representative to give you the idea.

The Cure

Basis of the Cure

As mentioned above, the basis for any reliable cure for hard-mouth—as well as for most other mouth problems—is *force-breaking*. The cure for hardmouth requires that the dog carry on command far longer than the non-force-broken dog would do voluntarily.

Curing the Chewer

For a dedicated Mallard-muncher, one that chews birds, and especially one that eats them, you need three special pieces of equipment: dead pigeons (frozen and unfrozen); a retractable lead; and an e-collar, preferably with momentary stimulation. (Your dog should be collar-conditioned before you start this cure.) *A chewer always rolls the bird before chewing it, so if you cure the roll, you automatically cure the chewing.* To cure the roll, you nick your dog with the e-collar every time he rolls the bird. Initially, you use frozen birds because they will hurt your dog's teeth if he chews them.

Until you have cured him in the backyard with this drill, do not let him retrieve birds in the field. Continue normal field training, but only with dummies. If you were to use birds in the field, his mouth problem would get worse instead of better, no matter what you might be doing in the backyard to cure it.

In the backyard, with your dog on lead and the e-collar around his neck, show him a frozen pigeon and tell him to *Fetch*. (Were he not force-broken, he very well might say, "Thanks a lot, but no thanks, Boss!" and refuse the bird. At best, he would carry it only as long as he wanted to, not as long as this cure requires.) Command *Heel* and start walking. Every time he starts to roll the bird in his mouth, nick him with the e-collar. Say nothing, do nothing, just nick him. Canine logic will eventually persuade him that rolling the bird causes the quick jolt on his throat. (If he were not force-broken, when nicked, he would probably spit the bird out and refuse to pick it up.) Through several short sessions, continue heeling him around the backyard, and continue nicking him every time he rolls the bird. When you get through an entire session, perhaps 10 minutes, without having to nick him, he is ready to advance.

Next, repeat the exercise, but with an unfrozen pigeon. Whenever he rolls it, nick him, and continue heeling him. If he would happen to

The author demonstrates the first step in curing the chewer of hardmouth with his Golden, "Gamble" (KC's Take'n A Chance WCX). Gamble is carrying a frozen (white) pigeon at heel while wearing the e-collar. (Gamble is not hardmouthed, and never has been. He is being framed, so to speak, by these pictures.) Photo by Theresa Spencer.

"attack" this bird too aggressively, go back to the frozen pigeon for a few minutes. That should settle him down a bit, after which you can again try the unfrozen pigeon. It may take several sessions, but eventually your dog will handle this bird gently. Of course, nick him whenever he rolls it. When you get through an entire session without having to nick him, he is ready to advance.

Next, after warming him up with a few minutes of carrying the unfrozen bird at heel, put him on your retractable lead. Now, toss the *frozen* pigeon a short distance and send him to retrieve it. Pay particular attention to how he picks it up, which is when most problems start. If he is at all rough with it, nick him repeatedly until he settles down. Also watch him carefully as he returns. Whenever he rolls the bird even slightly, nick him. It may take a few sessions, but eventually he will pick this frozen bird up politely and carry it back to you so gently that he wouldn't crack it if it were an egg. At that point, repeat these short backyard retrieves with the unfrozen pigeon, nicking him for "unnecessary roughness" both at the pickup and during the return. When he handles the unfrozen pigeon properly in these backyard retrieves, he is ready to advance.

Resume normal field work with birds, but keep the e-collar on him. Whenever he picks a bird up roughly, or rolls it on the return, nick him. He will eventually handle his birds, if not like eggs, at least

The author demonstrates the third step in curing the chewer or hardmouth with Gamble. He has tossed the frozen (white) pigeon in the backyard and sent Gamble to retrieve it. When doing this with your dog, you should pay particular attention to the pickup, for that's when most chewing starts. Photo by Theresa Spencer.

more gently than you ever dreamed he would. One more thing: Keep the collar on him during training for the rest of his active life, so you can correct him immediately should he ever backslide. For the same reason, hunt him with the e-collar on whenever you can do so safely, that is, without risk of the collar hanging him up in snags, tules, stick-ups and so forth.

How effective is this cure? I told you about my Shorthair, Erick, with the instincts of an 800-pound gorilla. Before starting this cure, he never brought me so much as an odd feather. He just consumed the bird where he found it. (As I said, I didn't let him continue this way. I stopped letting him retrieve birds in the field until I had cured him.) After curing him with this process, I began running him in AKC pointing breed hunting tests, first at the senior level and then at master level. Both levels require retrieving. He not only earned both titles without damaging a bird, but he occasionally brought me one that was still very much alive!

What kind of birds? Quail, the most fragile gamebird we have!

Curing the Flattener

The dog that *flattens but doesn't chew* birds is much easier to cure, provided you act immediately when he mangles the first one—even though it was an accident, as the first one usually is. If you let it go, the next "mishap" won't be quite so accidental, and so on until the habit becomes incurable. So act quickly, that is, the first time. (*Nota bene*: This drill won't work with the chewer; in fact, it would very quickly make his problem worse.)

You can cure this problem right out in the field, as soon as your dog flattens his first bird. When he delivers it, take it, show it to him, scolding him as you do. Then, command *Fetch* and make him take it again. Have him heel, carrying it, for a long time, in fact until he begs you to allow him to deliver it to you. (Were he not force-broken, you wouldn't be able to make him carry it any longer than he wanted to, which would make this cure impossible.) Give him a brief respite, and then make him carry it again for a long time. Through these protracted periods of uninterrupted carrying, you will make that smashed bird so repulsive to him that he will take pains not to flatten another one in the future. If you give him plenty of this medicine the first time, you probably won't have to repeat it again, at least not very soon.

Thereafter, take him off of retrieving birds for a couple of weeks. Use dummies in training. When you start him retrieving birds again, if he mashes another one—which is unlikely—repeat the process.

I used this technique with Misty (Weimaraner) back in the 1950s when she flattened the pigeon that flew out of her mouth in water. It was a hot July afternoon, and I heeled her for at least 30 minutes before giving her a break. Then, we did it again and again. I didn't let her retrieve for 30 days; and after that she never flattened another bird. But, thereafter, she did grip them more firmly.

My training buddy then, the late Sim Bowles, thought I was too severe with her, especially since she hadn't intended to mash the bird, just to catch it. But, without an immediate cure, she would have soon smashed another bird, and another, and another. Every flattened bird makes the cure that much more difficult, that much less permanent. In short, misguided "compassion" can make the problem incurable, and rather quickly at that. Realizing that, I cured her the first time, when it was easy.

STICKINESS

Perhaps I should start off by apologizing for even mentioning the word "stickiness" in polite retriever society. Most of us prefer not to think about it, much less talk about it. Why? Well, stickiness is to retrieverites what shanking is to golfers and what flinching is to shooters. None of us, including *moi*, knows all that much about it. So we view it somewhat superstitiously, fearing that if we so much as mention its name, this baffling affliction might visit our dogs.

Definition

What It Is

A sticky dog freezes, as if mesmerized, and refuses to release a bird. He holds it with a death-grip. He stares blankly with a bug-eyed expression. Anyone who has ever seen that look never forgets it.

The dog freezes so completely that the handler can, by raising the bird high enough, lift the dog off the ground. At a field trial once, pro D. L. Walters did exactly that. Lifting the duck up by its head, he dangled the dog off the ground until the bird separated at the neck. The dog tumbled to earth, still clutching the duck's torso. D. L. turned, handed the bird's head to one of the judges, shrugged, and said, "Sorry, but this is all I could get!"

In a multiple mark, a sticky dog will freeze only on the last bird retrieved. Intent on the remaining retrieves, he will release the other bird(s) readily. Thus, a knowledgeable handler can trick such a dog into releasing the last bird, at least occasionally, by pretending to send him for an imaginary blind retrieve. That little deception, first documented in the book *Charles Morgan on Retrievers*, worked for me many years ago, on the last bird of the last series of the last field trial in which I ran my Golden, Brandy. He had never stuck before, but one glance at his eyes told me what would happen if I tried to take that bird in the usual manner. Remembering Charley Morgan's suggestion, I put my left hand beside Brandy's head and whispered *Dead bird!* He came out of his trance, started looking for a blind retrieve picture, and released the bird easily when I said *Give*. You can't fool a dog that way often, but it can save the day on occasion.

What It Isn't

Stickiness is not a form of hardmouth. A sticky dog is almost never hardmouthed, almost never damages a bird. These are two separate—almost mutually exclusive—faults.

It is not an expression of dominance. True, a dominant dog that has not accepted the trainer as his pack leader will refuse to surrender birds. But he does not go into the hypnotic trance that characterizes true stickiness. In fact, he may growl when the trainer attempts to take the bird. And, if the trainer succeeds in prying it away, the dominant dog may attack! However, a venturesome trainer can cure this dog (not easily) by going back to basics and establishing his own dominance over the dog.

It is not an expression of possessiveness. Granted, some possessive dogs surrender birds reluctantly. But such dogs don't go into the hypnotic trance of true stickiness. You can overcome undue possessiveness *early* with consistent and copious petting and praising *before* taking the bird.

Causes

What causes true stickiness? My first inclination is to answer, "Beats the hell out of me!" But that isn't entirely accurate. I can identify some environmental factors which contribute to the problem. However, since these, neither individually nor collectively, produce stickiness consistently, they can only be "contributing factors," "triggering mechanisms," or "occasions of sin," not true causes. Thus, I suspect that the real cause is genetic, or at least partially genetic. That said, here are the contributing environmental factors of which I have knowledge.

Incomplete Force-Breaking

Many trainers, not all of them beginners, stress *Fetch* and slight *Give* during force-breaking. Their dogs come out of this process convinced that the former is a command, disobedience to which carries severe consequences. These same dogs tend to view *Give* more as a permission than a command. They feel they can release or not, depending on their own wishes at the moment. That, of course, sets up stickiness months or years later, after the trainer has forgotten how he force-broke the beast. How does a trainer instill this casual attitude toward *Give*? First, he praises on *Fetch* but not on *Give*, day in and day out. Second, when the dog refuses to release on command during force-breaking (as almost every dog does), the trainer doesn't take the disobedience as seriously as he does a refusal to *Fetch* on command. He repeats *Give* in a kindly voice. He may even pet the animal reassuringly as he does. The dog understands this as empowerment, giving him veto rights over *Give*. Later, when he doesn't want to release, he naturally assumes he has the right to refuse. *In my heart of hearts, I feel that incomplete force-breaking is the major contributing factor to stickiness.*

Poorly Timed Corrections

The trainer who punishes his dog—*for anything*—immediately after accepting delivery of a bird risks teaching stickiness. The dog reasons (quite accurately) that holding onto the bird can forestall a thrashing. Occasionally a novice trainer interprets the adage, "Don't punish a dog when he has a bird in his mouth," as an invitation to clobber the animal immediately after delivery. Dumb, dumb, dumb. A smart trainer corrects the miscreant rascal while he is actually misbehaving—whether or not he has a bird in his mouth—not later, and especially not immediately after he has done something right, like deliver a bird.

Sloppy Handling at Delivery

The trainer who habitually yanks birds from his dog's mouth can bring on stickiness. Instead of pulling on the bird, the handler should grasp its head, command *Give*, and insist that the dog release his grip and *back off.* The bird's body will then drop, hanging from his hand. If the dog releases but doesn't back off, the trainer should bump him in the chest with his knee—as firmly as necessary. After a few such bumps, the dog will release and back off as he should.

I frequently end training sessions with a few break-and-chase fun dummies. Using two dummies, I toss one as the dog delivers the other. All in one motion, I snatch one from the dog as I throw the other. Because the new throw distracts the dog from my manner of taking the other dummy, this casual approach works fine with two dummies. However, while hunting pheasants in Iowa a few years ago, I found it doesn't work with *one* bird. After he delivered the first rooster, I gave my Springer, Flick, a few extra fun-dummy-type retrieves with it. Each time he returned, I snatched the bird quickly and tossed it again. On the third such retrieve, Flick stuck! Not noticing it, I almost threw him with the bird. Then, looking at his eyes, I saw that unmistakable hypnotic stare. I stopped pulling on the bird, brought him back to reality by commanding

Hup! (which to a spaniel means *Sit!*) and then *Give!* with all the authority I could muster. He delivered nicely. He has never stuck again—and I have never snatched another bird from his mouth, believe me.

Training Pressure

The overly demanding trainer who keeps constant pressure on his dog test after test, session after session, month after month, risks stickiness. The dog may try several ploys to escape the pressure: no-go's; whistle refusals; bolting; water refusals; and refusing to release a bird. Too often, the trainer responds to each ploy with still more pressure—perhaps until the dog folds completely. Better by far, he should ease off a bit, let the dog have a few good days between pressured sessions. He should also relax a bit himself, for dogs pick up their trainers' tensions, too.

Dog-Game Conditions

Retrievers that regularly run in field trials and hunting tests are exposed to a lot of excitement from the crowd and other dogs, plus a lot of pressure from the challenging tests. Through all this they spend most of their non-working time confined in small crates and dog boxes— while traveling, overnight at motels, day after day on the trial or test grounds. Any half-bright dog figures out that as soon as he delivers the last bird of each series, the boss will stuff him back into his stall, usually leaving him there for several hours. No wonder an occasional retriever goes stir-crazy and sticks on the last bird of a test! Frankly, I think that was Brandy's problem when he stuck in his last trial.

Pointing breed dog-gamers handle this so much better. Instead of keeping their dogs in crates on the trial grounds, they stake them out on short chains. That allows each dog to move around, relieve himself, get water, relax, and enjoy life. This would work for retrievers, too, if they were staked where they couldn't see tests before running them.

The Cure

Prevention

With this problem especially, an ounce of prevention is worth a pound of cure. To prevent stickiness, avoid the above environmental factors.

Beyond that, you should learn to recognize the distinct "hypnotic stare." Talk to enough pros and you will find one that has such a dog around his place. Go and take a look. You won't forget that bug-eyed expression. Then, if you recognize it in your dog, you won't try to pull the bird from his mouth—even the first time. You will, instead, bring him out of his trance. In training, with a first-time offender, you can usually do this better by kindness than firmness. In a dog-game, you'll have to resort to what the British call "low cunning," like the *Dead bird* gimmick mentioned above. But only when your dog is back in the real world will he surrender the bird. Immediately thereafter, you should, of course, put him up, go home, figure out what created the problem, and how you can avoid it in the future.

But if prevention doesn't work—if your dog begins to stick habitually—you must cure him.

The Electronic-Collar Cure

As soon as your dog begins sticking, put an e-collar on him, preferably one with continuous stimulation. (Of course, he should have already been collar-conditioned.) With the collar in place, you can reinforce the *Give* command electronically. Use enough juice to get your dog's full attention immediately—in other words, go up a couple of levels above his norm. If you start this immediately after he sticks the first time, and if you follow through consistently in training, you will prevent him from slipping into this baffling habit.

Pre-Electronic Collar Approaches

Before the e-collar, trainers improvised all sorts of cures. Most of them were pretty rough, and none of them worked very well. Let me tell you about a few of them, so you can better appreciate what a fine training tool the modern e-collar is.

One pro hooked up a car battery to metal mesh doormat, which he placed beside himself, where the dog sits when delivering. If a dog stuck, the pro energized the mat, giving the animal enough juice to start a car engine. Results? Sticky dogs refused to sit at heel, even when he buried the mat under loose dirt.

Years ago, I helped a training buddy with a sticky Lab. He had me stand behind him at the line with a cattle prod. Whenever his dog stuck, my buddy nodded at me. That was my signal to jab the prod into the dog's rump and push the button, thereby giving the dog quite a jolt. (My buddy's theory was as follows: In field trials, a judge always stands behind the handler at the line; in training, I stood where the judge stands in trials, and I applied the prod when the dog refused to release a bird; canine logic would make him expect the judge do the same in a trial.) That approach helped get the animal through a trial now and then, but not consistently. It definitely didn't cure him. Nor did it endear me to this big, strapping young Lab. Every time I jabbed him with the prod, he released the bird, then looked around at me as if to say, "Someday, ole buddy, it's gonna be *your* rump and *my* teeth." Fortunately, dogs are very forgiving, so he never followed through.

Another pro worked out a technique he could use surreptitiously in trials. In training, *on only the last bird of each test,* he changed his method of taking the bird. He turned to face the dog, and as he grasped the bird, he dragged his right foot back a few inches. If the dog stuck, the trainer held onto the bird and booted the beast like a football. Ka-Boom! This looked like a sports blooper, in which a field goal kicker missed the ball and kicked the holder. In trials, on the last bird of each series, he repeated this procedure (*sans* kick). It intimidated the dog into releasing the bird, at least sometimes. Since shuffling his right foot back a little couldn't be interpreted as a "threatening gesture," judges couldn't penalize him for this. But it didn't cure the dog of stickiness—nor did it work consistently in trials.

Make-Do Techniques for Hunting

If you are hunting with your dog and he is not wearing an e-collar, you can extract birds from his locked jaws with the following two "work-around" measures. *These are not cures.* They will get you the bird, but won't address the underlying problem.

If you blow sharply in your dog's ear or nose (your choice), you will usually distract him enough to relax his jaws. Or, if you grasp the dog's upper thigh, poking your fingers into the groin area, and lift, he will usually release the bird. You cannot use these techniques in field trials or hunting tests because the rules forbid touching your dog while under judgment.

SLOPPY MOUTH

Definition

A sloppy-mouthed dog potters around while picking a bird up and then, while returning, repeatedly drops it and picks it up again. Such work looks bad and wastes time. This is an hereditary fault, from which the Golden Retriever suffers more than most. When you hear a Golden breeder say (usually with inexplicable pride), "Dogs of my breeding are soft-mouthed to a fault," the fault he is referring to is sloppy-mouth. Even so, with training, you can bring *most* sloppy-mouthed dogs up to an acceptable—although perhaps not a scintillating—performance level.

The Cure

The E-Collar Cure

You should first address the sloppy pick-up and then extend the training to the sloppy return. To do this, you should use an e-collar, preferably with continuous stimulation, in the following force-breaking drill. Obviously, your dog should be both force-broken and collar-conditioned before you start.

Lay out three or four dummies in the backyard. Having multiple dummies from which to choose will tempt him to "shop around," picking up and dropping one after the other. That will give you plenty of opportunities to convince him he shouldn't do that, that he should instead pick one up quickly and return with it.

Heel your dog, on lead, toward the dummies. When you are close to them but still moving, command *Fetch*, and start (mild) continuous stimulation. As soon as he picks up a dummy, stop the stimulation. If he drops it again, start continuous stimulation until he again has a dummy in his mouth (whether the same one or not doesn't matter). Now, with the lead, guide him back to you. Repeat this several times per session. Eventually, he will snatch up the first dummy he comes to and ignore the others.

Next, still in the backyard, put him on the retractable lead and toss a dummy. Send him. If he potters at all before picking it up, start continuous stimulation—but *say nothing*. (Were you to give him a *Fetch* command, he might form the habit of standing over birds and dummies until you say *Fetch*. That you don't want.) After going through the previous step, he will get the idea and snatch up the dummy without any further hesitation. If he drops the dummy while returning to you, zap him until he has again picked it up. Again, *say nothing*. Repeat this through several sessions until he neither potters before picking the dummy up nor drops it on the return. Then go back to normal retrieving in the field, and zap him whenever he slips back into any bad habits.

Clipped-Wing Pigeons

Here's another technique that will at least improve your dog's pick-up, although it won't cure sloppy-mouth like the above e-collar approach does. In training, use "clipped-wing" pigeons (hereafter called "clips"), much as spaniel trainers do to encourage a vigorous flush. (For directions on how to turn a normal pigeon into a clip, see Appendix I.) A clip cannot fly far. Mostly it will flutter up, flap, and run away from an indecisive dog. This encourages the dog to snatch the bird up first and think about it later.

Go to a field with cover light enough so your dog won't easily lose sight of the fluttering and running bird. Set up a short, simple single mark, and have your thrower toss a clip. When the bird comes down, send your dog. If he potters around, he won't catch it. He will have to chase it again and again and again, until he decides to dive in and grab it—which he will do, eventually, if he is birdy enough to bother with.

With a sloppy-mouthed dog, you should use clips as often as possible. They won't solve the problem all by themselves, but once you've cured him with the e-collar, they will give him plenty of "positive reinforcement" to persist in his new scoop-em-quick skills. Since clips will often flutter away if the dog drops them while returning, they also encourage him to hold them firmly on the way back to you.

POOR DELIVERY

Definition

A retriever should deliver to hand. He should carry the bird all the way to the handler, sit at heel, and hold it until told to release it. On command, the dog should release his grip on the bird and back off. *Anything short of that is poor delivery.*

How do dogs fall short? Some play keep-away, either by staying just out of the handler's reach or by deftly avoiding their handlers' hands after approaching close enough for delivery. Some drop birds before reaching their handlers. Some drop birds at their handlers' feet. Some "playfully" struggle to hold on as the handlers take the birds. Some release fine, but jump at birds after delivery. And so on.

A special delivery problem exists in water work. Without train-ing to the contrary, most dogs stop on shore, drop their birds, and shake the water from their coats. Many will abandon birds there and come in "empty." at least sometimes. Such a dog seems to say, "Boss, I got it this far without you. You can get it the rest of the way without me." Bad news, especially if you sink up to your knees in mud every step.

The Cure

Force-Breaking

Regardless of which delivery problem your dog exhibits, you can cure it through force-breaking. In fact, the only way to get *reliable* deliv-ery to hand—every bird every time—is through force-breaking. Once your dog is force-broken, most delivery problems will disappear, if you simply insist that your dog come in, sit at heel, and hold the bird or dummy until you command *Give*. That's why most serious retriever trainers routinely force-break every dog.

However, reliable delivery from water deserves special attention. With a force-broken dog, you can deal with drop-and-shake easily. If your dog drops the bird to shake immediately after landing, simply command *Fetch* and he will pick it up again and bring it to you. Better yet, before he drops the bird, command *Fetch* and toot the *Come-in* whistle. He will hang on and keep coming toward you. However, he may shake water from his coat "on the fly," so to speak, by shaking as he runs toward you. If he does this, and if you fear damage to birds, teach him to shake on command. Then you can insist that he come to you and deliver before shaking. He will shake all over you, of course, but this was your idea, remember.

To teach him to shake on command, say *Shake* every time he shakes water from his coat. The earlier in his life you start this, the better. In time he will associate your word with his action. If you continue this long enough and consistently enough, you will condition him to shake on "command." Then, when he lands with a retrieve, simply tell him *No* if he shakes on the shoreline, toot the *Come-in* whistle, and after he delivers, say *Shake*. This is training the easy, no-pressure way—by association, just as Pavlov did it. And it works, if you are consistent and persistent.

VOCALIZING

Definition

In waterfowl hunting, a noisy dog can cost a person a lot of opportunities to shoot birds, and can also cost a person a lot of hunting buddies, most of whom would rather shoot birds than listen to a canine concert. If the owner participates in any of the various off-season dog-games—hunting tests, field trials, working certificate tests—his loud-mouthed dog will cost him a lot of wasted entry fees, a lot of fruitless trips, and considerable embarrassment. In short, no one loves a noisy dog.

Dogs make noise in many ways. They bark, whine, yap, yodel, bay, yelp, and sometimes they emit sounds too unearthly for written approximation. Here, for simplicity's sake, I lump all audible canine oral outputs together as *vocalizing*. The precise type of sound matters far less than *when* the dog makes it—before the falls, during the falls, or after the falls. The first two are absolute show-stoppers. The last varies from a "so what?" to a major problem. Let me explain.

In hunting, some dogs become so excited at the sight of incoming birds that they vocalize, and thereby frighten the birds away. In dog-games, some dogs become so excited on the way to the line that they start vocalizing either en route or as soon as they reach the line—and the judges drop them for unacceptable hunting behavior. Dogs that vocalize during the falls are only slightly less objectionable, and will, if not checked, vocalize sooner and sooner until they do so at the first sight of birds.

After the falls, vocalizing may or may not be a problem. Many very stylish retrievers yelp softly when sent for a bird. A lot of folks disagree with me, but I not only don't object to this, I actually like it. It tells me the dog wants to retrieve so much he can hardly contain himself. Besides, what harm could it possibly do in a hunting situation? You and your buddies have just emptied your guns at a flock of birds. Some fell. Others flew away, terrified. No birds remain in the area for your dog to frighten with a little yelp as you send him. Over the years, I've had an occasional dog that yelped as he took off. These have been very stylish, very birdy. In his youth, Flick, my aging Springer, sometimes did this. I grinned every time he did. As I said, I like it. When judging retriever and spaniel hunting tests, I have heard many a yelp, and always from the better dogs. I have never penalized a dog for it. (Perhaps I should warn you that most other judges disagree with me on that point.)

However, I speak here of *just one little yelp*, no more. I have seen dogs that vocalized all the way to the bird. To me, that is totally unacceptable. Retrievers are supposed to be quiet dogs. Anyone who enjoys whistle-while-you-work dogs should try chasing hounds, which have much better voices, I'm told.

The Cure

Preliminaries

You should first teach your dog to *Hush* on command. Most city-dwelling dog-owners must do this to maintain peace and tranquility with their neighbors. For this, as I explained in *Training Retrievers for the Marshes and Meadows*, I reinforce the command *Hush* with a squirt of water from a plastic bottle. I also introduce the dog to the electronic bark collar when he reach about six months of age. That not only keeps him quiet at home, but it also accustoms him to electricity, and thereby prepares him for the e-collar.

The E-Collar Cure

In general, if your dog vocalizes—before the falls, during the falls, or after the falls—you should simultaneously nick him with momentary stimulation from the e-collar and say *Hush* every time he makes a sound. To use this approach, you must have previously collar-conditioned your dog. If you persist in this, he will figure out that you are serious.

The Electronic Bark Collar Cure

Here's another approach: Put a (waterproof) electronic bark collar on him before you heel him to the line. Of course, he should first have worn one around home enough to understand what starts and stops the stimulation. In training, let the collar do the work for you. Leave the collar on for the entire test, rather than removing it at the line.

If you opt for this approach, don't stop using the bark collar too soon—lest you make your young Caruso collar-wise. Use it every training session, every hunting trip, until vocalizing "has ceased to be a problem" (if I may borrow a line from an old Preparation-H ad).

Non-Electronic Cures

To cure a dog that vocalizes only after being sent, try this: As soon as he yelps, call him back to you, by hollering *No! Heel!* When he sits beside you again, scold him and perhaps shake his muzzle as you say *Hush!* Then send him again. Since the bird is already down, he won't become overly excited when sent the second time. He'll, as they say, go quietly. Good! Let him go. Enough of this and he will figure out that he only gets to complete the retrieve when he leaves quietly.

If he vocalizes before or during the falls, you might be able to cure him with the following admittedly slow and tedious, but non-electronic, approach. During training sessions, if he vocalizes as you heel him to the line, command *Hush* and squirt him in the face with water from your squirt bottle. If he quiets down, keep moving toward the line. If he continues to vocalize, squirt him again, shake his muzzle, and loudly proclaim any thoughts you may have about his ancestry. Now, *heel him back away from the line*. If possible, make him sit and watch another dog work. You may have to squirt and shake him as he watches. Good.

Marilyn Corbin and Summer demonstrate the use of a squirt bottle in quieting a dog that's noisy at the line. (Actually, Summer is not and never has been a "talker." On the other hand, Marilyn definitely is . . . but that's another story.)

Eventually, he will learn that he can get all the way to the line only if he keeps his mouth shut. Even then, he may vocalize at the line. If he does, show your displeasure and heel him back off the line again. Let him watch another dog work. Enough of this and he will—accidentally or on purpose—remain silent until the bird falls all the way to the ground. Great! Send him as quickly as you can. He deserves a reward. If you follow this procedure regularly, he will eventually figure out how to earn that reward.

But the e-collar will accomplish the same thing a lot quicker.

4
Single Mark Lengthening Drills

After your puppy is delivering to you reliably in the backyard and has been introduced to throwers, you should begin to lengthen his retrieves. Since most of us have relatively small backyards, that means going somewhere else to work. However, it doesn't mean going to a field with cover and other hazards. Until you have lengthened him out on land to at least 100 yards, you should work exclusively on "bare ground," as defined in Chapter 2.

Similarly, after your pup is swimming comfortably and doing puppy retrieves in water, you should begin to lengthen his water retrieves, but you should proceed very carefully, lest the length intimidate him into a no-go. You really don't need no-go's, especially at this early stage of training.

This chapter offers two drills for lengthening the youngster's retrieves: one for land, and the other for water.

DRILLS

Lengthening on Land

This trial-and-success drill is as plain-Jane as drills come. Being run on bare ground with highly visible white dummies, it doesn't challenge the dog's marking ability even slightly. In fact, all it does is accustom a young retriever to longer and longer retrieves in a fail-proof environment. Your thrower remains in one place, repeating the same throw over and over. In the first session, you set your dog up initially about 20

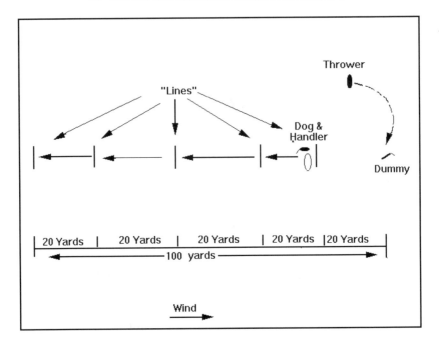

Figure 2. Lengthening on Land.

yards from your thrower. For each subsequent retrieve, you move back so as to make it about 20 yards longer than its predecessor. In each subsequent training session, you make the initial retrieve longer. After a few sessions, your pup will be totally comfortable running 100 yards (or more) on his initial run. With highly visible white dummies on bare ground, your dog always succeeds, so he builds confidence in his ability to complete longer and longer retrieves.

Purpose of Drill

Beginning golfers fear the long par-5 holes, especially after they have "blown up" on them repeatedly (as most beginners do). Similarly, inexperienced retrievers can develop a fear of long retrieves if they fail too often on them. The dog will indeed fail often if his trainer lengthens his retrieves out rapidly in cover while adding other hazards. After many failures, the dog learns that the longer the test, the less likely he is to find the bird. Small wonder, then, that some dogs despair, and no-go, whenever a test is longer than, say, 50 yards, regardless of how simple it might be.

To prevent your youngster from developing this fear of long

retrieves, you should introduce length first, on bare ground, and as a separate "hazard," before moving into cover. That's precisely what this drill does. Your dog will succeed many times in long retrieves on bare ground with highly visible white dummies, which are conditions that make failure virtually impossible. Then, after he is comfortable with extremely long retrieves, you can shorten up, move into cover and lengthen him out again without bringing on a bugaboo about length.

Prerequisites

Your dog should be accustomed to throwers.

Equipment and Facilities

You need an assistant with a pistol to throw dummies. Optionally, you can use a multi-shot dummy launcher. But a single-shot dummy launcher wouldn't do for this drill, because you would have to interrupt the flow of the training after every retrieve to reload the launcher. You also need several white dummies. Later on you will also need some dark dummies.

You should have a training vest with a gamebag pocket large enough to hold the dummies your dog retrieves to you. Since you move farther back after each retrieve, you can't drop the dummies on the ground, where they would confuse your dog on subsequent retrieves.

You need a level bare-ground area of at least 100 by 30 yards. The wind should blow along its length, so you can run straight downwind.

Although not absolutely necessary, a few stakes to mark the lines (starting positions) from which you will run your dog would be most helpful. With them in place, you know precisely where to retreat for each successive retrieve.

Precautions and Pitfalls

As mentioned above, don't drop dummies on the ground near any of the lines. Even if you pick them up, they will leave scent that may distract your dog on his next, longer retrieve, when he must run right over that area.

Don't overwork your dog in any one session.

Process—Steps in Training

Set up your test up according to the diagram. (Run it downwind because running into the wind encourages quartering, which is undesirable in marked retrieves.) With your thrower in position, set your dog at the first "line," which should be make the retrieve about 20 yards long, and signal for a throw. Your thrower should toss a white dummy angled back 45 degrees away from you, so your dog will have to run past him. Send your dog (or let him break if he's not steady yet). Since the dummy is so close and so visible, he'll simply run out and pick it up. As he does, you should run back another 20 yards to the next "line" (see diagram). When he delivers, set him up at this greater distance, and rerun the test. Again, as he goes for the dummy, you should run back to the next "line," about 20 yards farther away. And so on, until he is running the full 100 yards, or whatever length you choose.

If possible, change locations each time you do this drill. The next time you do it, start out at about 35 yards. The time after that, start at 50 yards, and so on until you are running initially from your maximum distance and not retreating farther. Then, add this variation: After running initially with a white dummy, repeat the test at the same distance but with a (less visible) red, gray, or black dummy. This will teach your dog to keep running even when he cannot see the dummy all the way. Switch entirely to dark dummies when you feel your dog can handle it.

Addenda

It is important to encourage young dogs to drive deep rather than hunt short. That's why your thrower should toss the dummies angled back 45 degrees away from you. Your dog should learn to run well past the thrower to reach the dummy as early in life as possible. Later on, but not in this drill, you can mix up the throwing angles, some angled back, some "flat" (90 degrees), and a few (but not many) angled slightly in.

After your dog ho-hums retrieves at your maximum distance with dark dummies in this bare-ground drill, move into cover and shorten up. Repeat this same drill there in cover, but add length very cautiously at first—maybe only 10 yards at a time. A short success is better than a long failure.

If you introduce your youngster to length this way—by making it a separate issue—length alone will never intimidate him, as it does so many young dogs.

Lengthening in Water

This trial-and-success drill helps you lengthen your youngster's retrieves in water, which is a far more delicate task than lengthening them on land. Dogs being land animals—no gills—they get from one place to another more comfortably on terra firma than in H_2O. So, you should add length in water as imperceptibly as possible. Mostly you simply make your dog's normal water tests a little longer, and a little longer, and a little longer—with emphasis on the word "little."

However, if you wish, you can use this one drill to help things along. In it, you have your assistant throw a series of three singles for your dog, each one a little longer than its predecessor. Since you run from the same line each time, and your assistant remains in the same place, the changes in length should be so subtle that they don't traumatize your dog—as long as your assistant controls any urge he may have to see how far he can throw a dummy on the third mark.

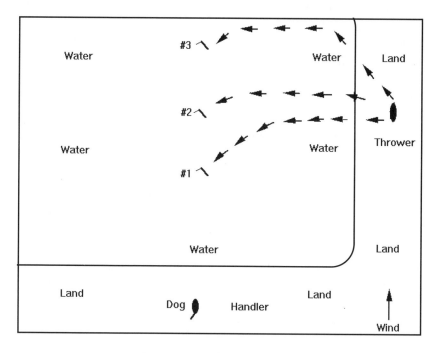

Figure 3. Lengthening in Water.

Purpose of Drill

This is an optional drill for lengthening a young dog's water retrieves.

Prerequisites

Your dog should be comfortable swimming and retrieving in water. He should have been introduced to throwers.

Equipment and Facilities

You need an assistant to throw dummies. A dummy launcher won't suffice for this drill because the throws require three different angles. You need three white dummies.

You need a pond where you can give your youngster a "square" (90-degree) entry into the water. That will prevent bank-running. The pond should be mostly open water, without snags and cover patches. At this stage, you don't need hazards.

Precautions and Pitfalls

Don't make any of the retrieves so long that your pup may become frightened and refuse to go (no-go). At this stage of training, you cannot correct him for no-go's, so avoid them. If in doubt about the length of a retrieve, shorten it up until your doubt is gone. If your dog enters the water reluctantly on either the first or the second retrieve, don't give him the remaining one or two. Change locations and shorten up before continuing.

Don't overwork your dog in any one session. Three retrieves are plenty in this drill.

Process—Steps in Training

Set the test up according to the diagram. Your thrower should stand in the same place for all three throws. He should toss the first dummy angled 45 degrees "in" (toward you). He should throw the second one "flat" (90 degrees), and the third one 45 degrees "back" (away from you).

In each retrieve, your dog should swim out, pick up the dummy, and return to you with it. Each time he reaches the dummy, praise him profusely, and continue doing so as he returns. However, when he is swimming out toward the dummy, remain silent, lest you distract him from his work.

Addenda

If your youngster is not yet force-broken, he will almost certainly stop near shore, drop the dummy, and shake the water from his coat. To prevent this while he is very small, meet him at the water's edge and take the dummy before he can drop it. Later, when he's a little bigger, just before he reaches shore, start running away from him, clap your hands, and talk excitedly to him. In his eagerness to catch you, he will probably forget about stopping, dropping, and shaking.

5
Single Mark Marking Drills

Anyone experienced in the ways of retrievers will tell you that marking is in the genes, that no amount of training can turn a lousy marker into a great one, or even into a passable one. Very true. However, unless a dog has adequate opportunities—through training sessions and work afield—to develop whatever innate marking talents nature has provided him, said gifts of nature will lie dormant and eventually atrophy. Furthermore, the right kind of training can contribute substantially to maximizing a dog's hereditary abilities, be they great, mediocre, or poor.

Toward that purpose, this chapter offers five marking drills. The first, "Reruns," is basic—*sine qua non* (without which there is nothing)—to all training in marking (and blind retrieves, for that matter). The second, "Salting," helps the beginning retriever learn to identify the area of a fall. The third, "Walking Marks," has two purposes: to encourage the inexperienced dog to run to the mark without going first to the thrower; and to give an experienced dog a series of challenging singles. The fourth and fifth, the "Laman Drill" and the "Stanfield Drill," encourage experienced dogs to pay closer attention to the falls.

[*Verba sapientibus*: Another drill which improves marking in most dogs is D. L. Walters' blind retrieve casting drill, "Walking Baseball," which is covered in the companion volume, *Retriever Training Drills for Blind Retrieves*.]

DRILLS

Reruns

Although, as mentioned above, reruns are basic for all parts of retriever training, we here discuss their role only as a trial-and-success drill for single marked retrieves. That role can be stated most simply as follows: *You should rerun every single mark with which your dog has the slightest difficulty.* If he doesn't "pin" it . . . "button" it . . . "step on" it . . . or whatever other "in" term you prefer for a perfect job, rerun the test immediately. If he has difficulty with it on the rerun, rerun it again—and so on, until he does indeed pin it. Of course, you shouldn't wear him out in any one session. If he tires before you accomplish what you want, rest him appropriately (even overnight) before continuing.

Purpose of Drill

The purpose of a rerun is to "calibrate your dog's marking eye," so to speak. On the initial run, he watched the fall from the line, but had difficulty finding it. Eventually, with or without help, he did indeed find it. So now he knows precisely where it fell. On the rerun, he again sees the same fall from the line, but this time he knows exactly where it is landing. Thus he subconsciously adjusts (fine-tunes) his "mark" for this fall. If you rerun him regularly on challenging marks, he will tend naturally to generalize this fine-tuning operation.

When a rifleman sights in his new rifle, he shoots at the bull's-eye of the target. Then he checks out where the bullet actually struck. If it hit a few inches below the bull's-eye, he adjusts his sights downward so the cross-hairs mark the spot where the bullet hit the target. Ditto if the bullet hit high or to either side. Wherever the bullet struck the paper becomes the "reality" to which he adjusts his sights. Then, when he again puts the cross-hairs on the bull's-eye and pulls the trigger, the bullet does indeed strike the paper where the sights indicate it will. Similarly, a retriever adjusts his marking eye to reality by rerunning tests. On the initial run, he locates the spot where the dummy fell. On the rerun, he corrects his perception of the fall from the line. When he runs to the spot where he has now marked the fall, the dummy is indeed there. This run/rerun process not only allows him to adjust his sights appropriately, but it also gives him confidence in his marking ability.

Prerequisites

Reruns have no special prerequisites beyond those of the original run of the same test.

Equipment and Facilities

In rerunning a test, you need only what you had for the initial run, whatever that may have been.

Precautions and Pitfalls

Don't waste time rerunning tests your dog aces the first time. His marking eye needs no fine-tuning on those. (If he pins most of his marks, either he is a marking phenom, or your tests are too easy.)

On the rerun, everything should be the same as it was on the initial run. Any significant variation will confuse rather than help your dog.

Don't overwork your dog in any one session.

Process—Steps in Training

Simply rerun the test as-is until your dog masters it, being careful not to overwork him in any one session.

Rerun the test *exactly* as you originally ran it: same line, same thrower position; same throw, with the dummy landing in the same place. If on the rerun the dummy lands a significant distance from where it fell on the original run, don't send your dog. Instead, call "No Bird!" Your thrower should then pick the dummy up, return to his throwing position, and, on your signal, throw it again, this time so it falls where it fell on the previous run. Incidentally, when you are throwing for someone else, don't take these "No Bird!" calls personally. The handler at the line is training his dog, not critiquing your throwing arm.

Should your dog fail to find the dummy in the initial run (or any subsequent run, for that matter), you should deal with it as recommended in *Dealing with Loose Hunts in Training* in Chapter 2.

Addenda

Rerunning is the essence, the heart and soul, of drilling. If you don't rerun an exercise, you aren't drilling. Thus, I have been astounded in recent years to hear a few prominent pros arguing against rerunning marks. They claim that, in multiple marks and in mixed mark-and-blind tests, reruns incline dogs to return to old falls. Although this claim is true, it's also absolutely irrelevant! With or without reruns, dogs are genetically inclined to both switch and return to old falls. This undesirable inclination is just part of "the nature of the beast." So, whether rerun or not, every dog must be trained not to switch and not to return to old falls (see Chapter 9, *Double Mark Switch-Proofing Drills*). After being so trained, he won't commit these errors, whether rerun or not.

One pro has offered another—and even more inane—argument against reruns. He said he had been unsuccessful in training one particular dog that had been rerun on marks regularly before coming to him for training. He claimed that, as a result of these reruns, this dog wouldn't try on the first run, because he knew he would get a second chance. Let's look at two gaping holes in that argument. First, every retriever worth training has an insatiable desire to retrieve. It's a mania with them, not something they can turn on and off. If that one dog so lacked this basic instinct that he didn't care enough to try on his first run, why would he give a damn on the rerun? Second, this pro has received hundreds, perhaps thousands, of partially trained dogs for training. Unquestionably, before coming to him, many (probably most) of them had been routinely rerun. Out of all those dogs, he claims that only one suffered this problem. Wouldn't it be more reasonable to suspect that this particular dog had weak marking genes, that nothing could make him more than a miserable marker? All dogs do better on reruns (but genetically poor markers don't learn much from them). Thus, this pro has erroneously attributed this particular dog's improved work on reruns to greater effort instead of greater familiarity with the particular test.

In years past, every pro of my acquaintance spent a lot of time convincing unwilling beginners to rerun tests. I've heard beginners spout all sorts of lame excuses, some even weaker than those cited above. And I've heard pros patiently persuade them that reruns, although perhaps not always exhilarating for trainers, help the dogs immensely. Why the recent change of attitude in at least a few pros?

One anti-rerun pro perhaps inadvertently let the cat out of the bag. He said he opposes reruns "because I want to spend as much time training my good dogs as I do training my lesser dogs." Reruns take time. They make it impossible for a pro to devout equal time to each dog. Most pros want to be fair with their clients, that is, give each one the same amount of training for their money.

(Besides, a pro who doesn't rerun tests can add more dogs to his string, and thereby increase his income. Of course, training each dog takes longer overall, because the needed repetitions must come in subsequent training sessions. But, most pros are workaholics. They typically conduct two training sessions per day, one lasting all morning, the other all afternoon. They do this six or seven days a week, for ten or eleven months a year. With so much training time, a pro can still train each dog, without reruns, more rapidly than the average amateur can train his own dog, with reruns, because most amateurs train only three or four times a week—mostly during the months of daylight savings time.)

If you're a pro, by all means eliminate reruns in order to divide your time equally among your dogs and to maximize the size of your string. But have the decency to state clearly why you're doing it. Don't confuse beginners with a lot of nonsense about "returning to old falls," and "not trying on the initial run."

On the other hand, if you are *not* such a pro, don't let anyone talk you out of the benefits regular reruns offer for improving your dog's marking. Enough said.

"Salting"

The term "salting" originated during the gold rush days, when hustlers, to sell worthless claims, would "salt" them with gold nuggets from productive mines. In this drill, the thrower "salts" a "productive mine" (the area of the fall) with several extra dummies to improve the dog's chances of finding one of them.

This is a trial-and-success drill for young or inexperienced retrievers, especially while they are being introduced to more and more challenging single marks. By putting several dummies in the area of the fall, you increase dramatically the probability that the youngster will find at least one of them. This enables him to experience success, which is especially important in the early stages of every phase of training. After only a few successive failures, many young dogs will so lose confidence in themselves that they no-go. Salting can prevent that.

It also offers a significant side benefit. Several dummies give off more scent than a single dummy. That extra scent helps the pup identify the area of the fall when he reaches it. This alone would make the drill worthwhile, for until the dog has developed confidence in his ability to find the area of the fall, he won't stay in it long enough to find the dummy. He'll give it a quick once-over, and then take off hunting here,

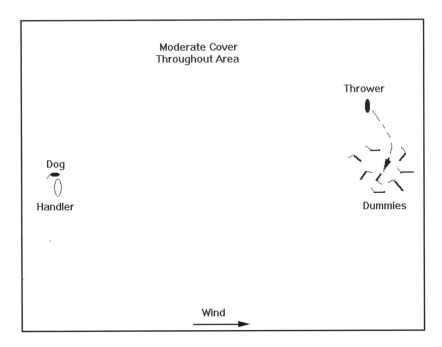

Figure 4. "Salting."

there, and everywhere. But once he *believes* in his ability to find the area of the fall, he'll hunt right there until he comes up with the dummy.

Purpose of Drill

This drill both builds the dog's confidence in his own ability and helps him learn to identify the area of the fall. These two factors combined encourage the dog to persevere in hunting the area of a fall until he finds the dummy.

Prerequisites

You should begin using this technique as soon as you move from bare ground into cover.

Equipment and Facilities

You need an assistant with a blank pistol, or a dummy launcher. You need several dummies. In general, I recommend large black ones for this drill. When thrown, they show up well against almost any background, and when lying in cover, they are reasonably visible to the dog.

Thus, they encourage him to use his eyes as well as his nose. However, with a dog that is very unsure of himself, you may want to start out with several white dummies, which are even more visible. (If, when thrown, a white dummy doesn't show up well against the sky, throw dark dummies, but salt with white ones.)

Precautions and Pitfalls

Your dog will almost certainly "shop" a bit among the several dummies he finds in the area of the fall. By "shop" I mean he'll pick up and drop more than one dummy. He'll pick one up, start back toward you, then stumble onto another dummy. He'll probably drop the one he has and pick up the new one. He may go back and forth between the two of them. Then he may encounter a third, and so on. This can be irritating, but it should not be a major concern to you. Since you are using large dummies, he can't pick up more than one at a time. If you were using small dummies, he could pick up two or more—that could create a mouth problem you don't want. By using large dummies, you can relax and work him through this "shopping" hassle. As soon as he picks up a dummy—whether the first, second, or whatever—start tooting the *Come-in* whistle and clapping your hands. Even run away from him as you do this. Do whatever will encourage him to come to you promptly with whatever dummy he has at the moment. As an absolutely last resort, you could shorten up and put him on a retractable lead, which would allow you to lead him back to you as soon as he picks up the first dummy. (Here I'm assuming your dog has not yet been force-broken. If he has been, you can cure shopping through the "Sloppy-Mouth" cure in Chapter 4.)

But, no matter how frustrated you get with his shopping, don't correct him in any way. Don't holler at him. Don't have your assistant chase him toward you. Don't zap him with the e-collar. If you put him on the retractable lead, resist the temptation to jerk him back roughly. You are using this drill to build his confidence through trial-and-success. If you blow your stack, you'll also blow the benefits of the drill.

Process—Steps in Training

Leave your dog in his crate while you set up the test. Position the thrower and have him toss a dummy where you want it to fall. Now have him go to the dummy and scatter a few (four to six) dummies around in the area of the fall. In doing so, he is "salting" the area. Each dummy should be at least five yards from any other dummy. Such separation better defines a reasonable area of the fall, and it discourages (although does not eliminate) shopping.

Now your assistant should return to his throwing position. Get your dog out of his crate, heel him to the line, set him up, and signal for a throw. When the dummy lands, send your dog. If he reaches the area of the fall, he will almost certainly find a dummy. For him that is a success—and success is what you seek in this drill.

If he can't find one—unlikely as that is—have your assistant help him out. Then, immediately rerun the test. In fact, even if your dog finds a dummy on his own, but has some difficulty doing so, you should immediately rerun the test. For the rerun, you may want the area salted with more or fewer dummies, depending on how he did the first time. If he failed totally, you should put out more dummies for the rerun. If he did reasonably well, but shopped around too much, you might want to rerun the test with fewer salted dummies, or even with none at all.

Addenda

Salting is a confidence-builder for young or inexperienced dogs. You can use it whenever you increase the difficulty of the single marks you give your pup. Frankly, it's a crutch, designed to ensure initial success. Don't lean on it too long. As soon as your youngster is comfortable with a given test, discontinue salting on it.

If you have the facilities (cover patches in a body of water) you can also salt singles in water. However, after the test, you or your assistant will have to slog around in the tules, searching for and picking up the leftover dummies.

Walking Marks

In this drill, the thrower walks from one station to another, throwing a single mark from each one. While your dog is returning with the first retrieve, the thrower walks to a second location (pre-selected or random). And so on.

Purpose of Drill

You can use this drill for either of two purposes, one trial-and-success, the other trial-and-error. First (trial-and-success), if yours is a

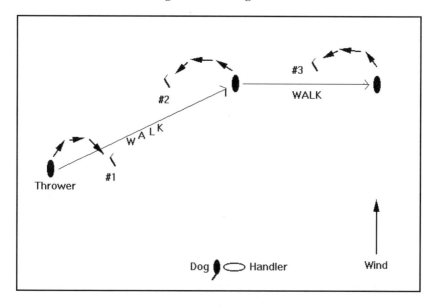

Figure 5. Walking Marks.

young dog that still tends to suck into the guns as he runs to his marks, this drill will help him overcome that problem. Have your assistant make all of his throws, after the first one, back toward his previous location. The attraction of the previous fall will offset that of the gun and help your dog run straight to his current mark. Second (trial-and-error), if yours is a more experienced dog that isn't concentrating on the falls as he should, this drill will give him a wake-up call. Have your assistant move from place to place, throwing a series of challenging singles, perhaps a little snug to one another. If your dog doesn't watch each one carefully, he may mis-mark it and return to the area of the previous fall. If he does, you should correct him. After a few corrections, he will pay better attention.

Prerequisites

Your dog should be doing singles in cover. (He should also have one of the problems for which this test was designed.)

Equipment and Facilities

You need an assistant with a blank pistol and several dark dummies. White dummies would be too highly visible. Your assistant needs some way to tote the dummies from place to place. A training or hunting vest would be ideal, but an old gunnysack will do.

If you are using this drill to sharpen up an experienced dog's marking, you need an e-collar, preferably with momentary stimulation. Although not absolutely necessary, a pair of two-way radios will facilitate communications between you and your assistant.

You need grounds appropriate for your dog's current needs.

Precautions and Pitfalls

Unless you are using two-way radios, you should, before starting, explain to your assistant where he should walk and where he should throw. This will eliminate the need for a lot of yelling and arm-waving between the two of you. Some dogs are intimidated when their handlers yell at assistants out in the field.

If you are using this drill to pull an inexperienced dog away from the guns, keep the marks simple and reasonably far apart. You are solving a problem created by a lack of confidence, so you want your dog to succeed quite easily on each retrieve.

If you are using this drill to sharpen an experienced dog's marking, you should give him challenging marks, but don't make them so tough that he fails consistently. Let him pick most of them up clean. Trap him just often enough to make the drill productive.

Don't overwork your dog in any one session.

Process—Steps in Training

If you are using this drill to pull an inexperienced dog away from the guns, run it according to the diagram. After throw #1, your assistant should walk toward and well past that fall, and then throw #2 back toward #1. But he should walk far enough so that the areas of the two falls are totally separated and distinct. After throw #2, he should walk away from that fall and then throw #3 back toward it. And so on.

If you are using this drill to sharpen up an experienced dog's marking, don't follow the walking/throwing pattern in the diagram. Instead, improvise your own so that you can maximize your use of the hazards in your grounds. Make each successive mark as tight with its predecessor as you feel your dog should be able to handle. Whenever he falls through the trapdoor, so to speak, and returns to the area of the previous fall, nick him with the e-collar, have the thrower help him out, and then rerun that particular mark before moving on.

Addenda

This drill makes highly productive use of your training time, because it requires little time to set up and execute.

Laman Marking Drill

Pro Jane Laman showed me this trial-and-error drill many years ago on one of the many high and steep hills near Manhattan, Kansas. The line is at the top of such a hill, and the series of three single marks are in the flat valley below. Each mark, after the first, is shorter than its predecessor. With the dog running full-tilt when he reaches the bottom of the hill, he will overrun the shorter marks unless he is really paying attention. After getting in trouble a few times for over-running, he will focus much more sharply on each fall and thereby mark the area much better.

Purpose of Drill

This drill motivates the inattentive dog to pay closer attention to each fall. In this way, it improves his marking, at least temporarily. Most

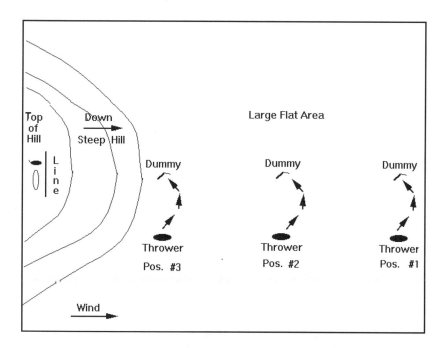

Figure 6. Laman Marking Drill.

experienced dogs become overconfident from time to time. Overconfidence leads to inattentiveness, which in turn leads to sloppy marking. This drill will take the ho-hum out of a dog's attitude at the line.

Prerequisites

The dog should be doing, as a minimum, significant single marks in cover. He should be steady. He should also have been collar-conditioned.

Equipment and Facilities

You need an assistant with a blank pistol and several dark dummies. White dummies would be too highly visible. You need an e-collar, preferably with momentary stimulation.

You need a high and steep hill with a flat valley beneath it. Throughout the area the cover should be light to medium with no significant hazards. You want a place where your dog can let out the stops and run! If you live in extremely flat country, skip this drill and use the Stanfield drill, which follows immediately.

Precautions and Pitfalls

When you correct your dog with the e-collar, go as lightly as possible, especially the first few times you run him on this drill. You want him to realize he has made a mistake, but you don't want to terrify him. This is one of the many situations in which a light, nagging correction, repeated through several sessions, will accomplish much more than a single "cure-all" jolt.

Don't overwork your dog in any one session.

Process—Steps in Training

[*Nota bene*: Throughout this drill, all throws should be "flat" (90-degree angle), to encourage overrunning.]

Your assistant should start at the farthest station, which should be at least 100 yards from the line, and 150 would be better. Set your dog up at the line and call for a throw. When you send your dog, he'll wheel merrily down the hill, sail across the flatlands, and scoop up the dummy. Great!

As he returns to you, your assistant should move in to the second station, which should be about halfway between the first station and the base of the hill. Again, call for a throw, and send your dog. This time he will almost certainly race past the dummy and return to the area of the first fall. When he gets there, nick him lightly with the e-collar, and then have the thrower help him out. Immediately rerun that mark. He should nail it this time.

As he returns to you, your assistant should move in closer, to station 3, which should be right at the base of the hill. Call for a throw and send your dog. After being propelled by gravity to the bottom of the hill, he will almost certainly fly past the dummy and return to the area of the previous fall. Again nick him lightly, have the thrower help him out, then rerun that mark.

On these reruns, you'll notice that your dog strains to focus on the fall. That's what you want from this drill. If you can locate several hills, run this drill from each one of them occasionally. After going through it a few times, your dog will focus much more tightly on every fall the first time. He'll know what you're setting him up for, and he'll be determined not to fall into the trap. Thus, he may get through the entire drill without a correction. Great! That's what you want—especially when you're preparing him for a test or trial.

Addenda

Like most marking drills, this one depends for its effectiveness on the inattentive dog's inclination to overrun a short fall, especially after picking up a longer one. This drill amplifies that tendency by starting the dog off running down a steep hill.

Stanfield Marking Drill

Pro Ron Stanfield taught me this trial-and-error drill a number of years ago. Like the Laman drill, it gives the dog a series of shorter and shorter marks, tempting him to overrun. However, you run this drill on flat ground—because Ron lives in the Texas flatlands. Some dummies are thrown left-to-right and others right-to-left. The throwing sequence makes three of the marks "gimme's" and the other two "gotcha's." This mix keeps the dog happy while inducing him to pay better attention to the falls.

Purpose of Drill

This drill encourages the dog to focus more intently on each mark.

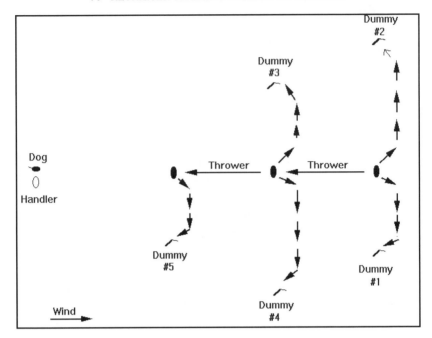

Figure 7. Stanfield Marking Drill.

As mentioned above, most dogs, as they gain experience in marking, become more and more confident—which is good. But increasing levels of confidence leads invariably to overconfidence—which is bad. Like the Laman drill, this one gives such a dog a wake-up call.

Prerequisites

The dog should be doing significant single marks, and should be steady. He should have been collar-conditioned.

Equipment and Facilities

You need an assistant with a blank pistol and several dark dummies. White dummies would be too highly visible. You need an e-collar, preferably with momentary stimulation.

You need a large, relatively flat field, with light to moderate cover, at least 100 yards long (150 would be better), with the wind blowing along its length, so you can run with the wind. The flatter the ground and the lighter the cover, the more the dog will be inclined to lay his ears back and run. As long as the cover conceals the dummy, it is heavy enough. If you live in country too hilly for this drill, use the Laman drill, above.

Precautions and Pitfalls

In correcting the dog with the e-collar for overrunning, you should just nick him lightly. If you light him up like Times Square, you will create a hot-spot you don't want. Such a hot-spot could make it impossible to run this drill again in the same location for a while.

Don't overwork your dog in any one session.

Process—Steps in Training

[*Nota bene*: Throughout this drill, all throws should be "flat" (90-degree angle), to encourage overrunning.] Set this drill up so your dog runs downwind. Running into the wind not only encourages quartering, but also allows your dog to scent the dummy before he gets to it. Running downwind, he must mark it.

Position your assistant at the maximum distance (100 to 150 yards). He can throw the first dummy in either direction. The distance he throws this first one is not critical, but it will be very important on all subsequent throws. Send your dog. Next, your assistant should make a long throw (#2) in the opposite direction. As your dog returns with this second dummy, your assistant should walk straight toward you about one-third of the distance between you and him. From that position, he should next throw (#3) flat in the same direction as his second throw, but he should throw it only long enough so it falls approximately on the line between your dog and the #2 fall.

If your dog overruns this mark, let him run all the way to the area of the first mark before correcting him. Then nick him lightly with the e-collar, and have the thrower help him out. Rerun this third mark immediately.

Next, from the same position, your assistant should throw (#4) long and flat in the opposite direction. Your dog should pick this one up without incident, but if not, correct him, have the thrower help him. As he returns to you with the dummy, your assistant should walk in about half the distance between you and him.

Next, from this shorter distance, your assistant should throw (#5) in the same direction as #4, but just far enough so the dummy lands approximately on the line to the previous dummy. If your dog overruns this one, let him get all the way to the area of the previous fall before nicking him lightly. Then have the thrower help him out and rerun this mark.

Addenda

After you run your dog on this drill a time or two, he will catch on to it. Then he will begin concentrating more intensely on each mark—which is what this drill was designed to do for you. Thereafter, his marking in general will improve for a certain length of time. Thus, it's a good drill to run shortly before a trial or test.

If possible, run it in several different locations. Too many successive repetitions in the same place will lessen the effectiveness of the drill. Also, use different distances each time you run it. Start out sometimes at, say, 150 yards. At other times start at maybe only 85 yards. Start at 100 or 125 yards other times. This will change the distances for all the marks, which will prevent your dog from putting it on autopilot and running just so far on each mark in the series.

At the lengths proposed, only two marks (#3 and #5) are "gotcha's," on which the dog may get into trouble. The rest are "gimme's" that he should pick up without incident. That's a nice ratio. If you start out significantly longer, say at 200 yards, you should be able to squeeze in another "gotcha" and another "gimme." If you do, make sure you don't overwork your dog. He runs a long way every time you send him. If you have to correct him and rerun any of the marks, he runs that much more. So watch for signs of fatigue.

6
Single Mark Straight Line Drills

Is it necessary that your dog take straight lines to his marks? . . . straight lines through cover and terrain variations on land? . . . straight lines angling into water? . . . straight lines angling out of water? . . . straight lines in water past islands and points? . . . straight lines seemingly *ad nauseam* from the line to the bird? Frankly, the answer depends on "where you're calling from."

If you aspire to become a field trialer, the answer is an unqualified "Yes"—not only if you intend to run in the major stakes (open and amateur), but even if you'll settle for the minor stakes (qualifying and derby). Whether you like it or not, whether you agree with it or not, if you want to play the field trial game, you need a detour-free dog. To win, your dog must not "cheat," that is, run the bank, in water tests. Nor can he avoid hazards in land tests.

If you aspire to becoming a hunt tester, the answer is a qualified "Yes." In the lowest level, your dog *might* survive in spite of significant cheating. In the middle level, he *might* squeak by in spite of noticeably cheating. In the highest level, he *might* qualify in spite of a little minor cheating. But in all three levels, running "crooked" counts against him to some degree or another. Therefore, if on a given day your dog's work reveals a few other untidy edges, cheating could be the grease that sends him sliding down the tube. Besides, dogs don't understand the difference between a little cheating and a lot. In the black-and-white canine mind, cheating is either okay or it's not. So, if you have hunt test aspirations, you should train your dog not to cheat.

If you have no dog-game aspirations, but intend only to hunt with your retriever, the answer is a qualified "No." You'll seldom knock a bird down, whether in the marshes or meadows, that your dog can't pick up, no matter how crooked a path he takes to reach it. Granted, an occasional fall requires a reasonably straight line. For example, if by running the bank, the dog would put himself on the wrong side of a "hog-tight" fence blocking further access to the water, to reach the bird, he would have to take a reasonably straight line from your duck-blind into the water. Such things do happen, but too rarely, perhaps, to justify the time and effort necessary to train your dog to take straight lines, not to mention the time and effort to maintain that training. If you enjoy training, if it's your year-around hobby, by all means teach straight lines. Both you and your dog will enjoy it. But, otherwise, you can get by without it.

If you decide to teach straight lines, do it in a rational sequence of steps. We tend to think of cheating as a water-related problem, and it generally is, at least from a human point of view. However, dogs can't make such fine distinctions. They feel obliged to go straight either always or never. So you should teach straight lines on land, even if you don't really care about them. In fact, you should start there. If your dog first learns to run true on land, he will more easily understand the corrections he receives later for cheating in water. For such land training, this chapter has one drill, "Straight Lines Through Land Hazards."

After you attend to this initial indoctrination on land, you should use a logical series of steps to transfer this concept to water. Your dog can cheat in several ways. On his way to a bird, he can run down the shoreline rather than angle into the water. After he enters the water, he can go out of his way to land on a point or island between you and the bird. On the other side of the pond, he can suck into shore too soon instead of carrying an angled exit toward the bird. Then, too, he can make similar mistakes while returning to you with the bird. If you tried to address all of these possible errors at once, you would wind up punishing your dog so often that he would become bewildered, give up, and probably no-go. To avoid this, you should attack each of these types of cheating one at a time. Divide and conquer, so to speak—and of course, attack the simplest problem first. Start with "angled returns," that is, teaching your dog to return straight to you, even when that means swimming at an angle rather than cutting into the nearest point of land. Since he has already made the retrieve, you can correct him as he returns without creating a no-go problem. For teaching angled returns, this chapter has two drills, "Drill to Introduce Straight Water Returns" and "Dobbs Water Return Drill."

After he understands angled returns, teach him to take angles when going to a fall. These come in two flavors: angled entries, in which he must angle into the water after leaving your side; and angled exits, in which he must angle out of the water on the far shore. After he learns to take angles on the return, neither of these should present much risk of a no-go problem. This chapter offers one drill for each: the "Angle-In Drill" and the "Angle-Out Drill." Since these two are of about equal difficulty, you can teach them in either sequence.

Finally, you should train your dog to swim straight past inviting points and islands near his route to and from the bird. For this, this chapter has one drill, "Points and Islands Drill." When you complete all this work, your dog will not detour from his line to the bird, whether on land or in water. He will charge through hazards on land, angle into and out of the water, and thumb his nose at inviting points and islands as he swims past them.

DRILLS

Straight Lines Through Land Hazards

This drill uses the e-collar's hot-spotting technique to teach the dog to take straight lines through hazards on land. In the diagram, the hazard is an area of heavy cover in a field of light to moderate cover. However, the same technique can be used for other hazards, such as rolling ground, small hills, deep ditches, and so on.

You start out in trial-and-success mode and work gradually into trial-and-error mode. Initially, locate the line within the hazard, where your dog cannot avoid it, because he's already smack in the middle of it. This patterns him to go through rather than around. Then you move into trial-and-error mode by moving the line farther and farther back behind the hazard. Sooner or later, and probably sooner, your dog will detour around the hazard, either going out or coming back. When he does, nick him with the e collar at the widest spot on his "end-run." This will create a hot-spot there, which he will avoid on future runs. After some number of unpleasant end-run experiences on both sides of the hazard, your dog will churn straight through the middle like an enraged fullback.

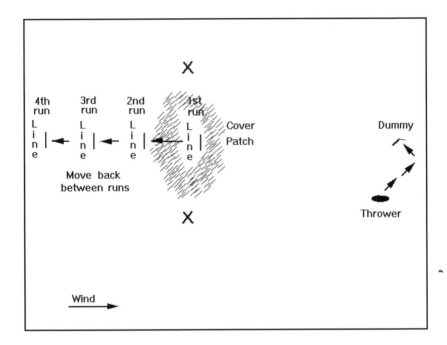

Figure 8. Straight Line Through a Land Hazard.

Purpose of Drill

This drill teaches the dog to run straight through rather than around various land hazards.

Prerequisites

Your dog should be steady and should be doing reasonably difficult single marks in cover. He should be collar-conditioned.

Equipment and Facilities

You need an assistant or multi-shot dummy launcher. With a single-shot dummy launcher, reloading after each run would destroy the rhythm of the drill. You need several dummies (of any sort you like). You need an e-collar, preferably with momentary stimulation.

You need an appropriate location, one with the type of hazard you wish to train your dog to run straight through. Ideally, your location will be rather ho-hum (light to moderate cover, level ground, and so forth) except for the one hazard.

Precautions and Pitfalls

The e-collar correction should be a single, quick nick, not a sustained zap. Don't nick your dog too close to the line, lest you create a no-go problem. Set the drill up so he will be at least 20 yards away from you before you have to nick him. This is a hot-spotting correction, in which you establish a place for him to avoid, so nick him only when he reaches the widest point in his detour around the hazard (point X in the diagram).

Make the mark very simple, one your dog can find quite easily after getting through the hazard. It would be highly counterproductive if your dog were to get into trouble on the mark after successfully negotiating the hazard.

Don't overwork your dog in any one session.

Process—Steps in Training

Trial-and-success phase: Set up your test with the initial line in the middle of the hazard. In his first run, he'll charge through the last half of the hazard, run out and pick up the dummy, and then return into the hazard, since you're still there. That will "pattern" him to go through the hazard on subsequent runs from behind the hazard.

Next, move the line back immediately behind the hazard. Since he starts out almost touching the hazard, he will almost certainly take the correct line. If he doesn't, don't nick him, since he's so close to you (and might no-go next time if you did). Instead, say "No!" Call him back, heel him a couple of steps into the hazard, and send him again.

Trial-and-error phase: After he has succeeded in going directly through the hazard from immediately behind it, move the line back another 15 or 20 yards. From here, your dog can see that he could easily run around the hazard. If he does so, either going out or coming back, nick him with the e-collar when he is at the widest point in his end-run (point X in the diagram). Say nothing. Do nothing. Let him complete the retrieve. Then heel him about 5 yards closer to the hazard, and rerun the test. If he makes an end run to the other side of the hazard, going or coming, nick him again at the widest point. Then rerun him from the same line. Chances are he will go straight through. If he doesn't, correct him the same way again, and try again, perhaps from a little closer.

Eventually he will run straight through the hazard to avoid the "bumblebees" he's encountered while running around it on either side.

When he goes through properly, move the line back another 10 or 15 yards and rerun the test. And so on, until he goes through the hazard from any reasonable distance behind it.

Addenda

To get your dog to run through such hazards *reliably*, you will have to repeat this drill in many places with many different hazards. But don't try to do it all at once. Mix in other kinds of work between sessions on these hazards.

Drill to Introduce Straight Water Returns

This drill is a trial-and-success preparation for the "Dobbs Water Return Drill." It begins by giving your dog a series of "square" exits on the two sides of a corner of the pond. After each throw, you run around the corner of the pond and encourage your dog to swim straight to you, even though you've moved from where you sent him. Since swimming straight to you doesn't involve an angle, your dog will do it without a

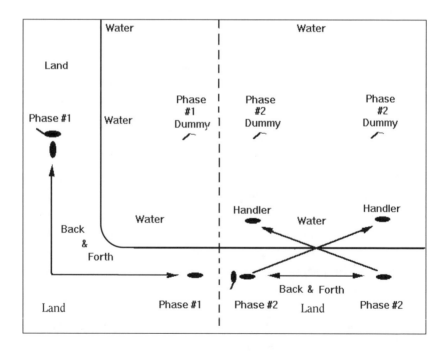

Figure 9. Straight Water Return (Introduction).

problem. A few of these will pre-condition him to swim to "where you are, not where you were."

Next, you give your dog a series of angled returns to you while you are standing in the water. Standing on shore with your dog sitting at heel, toss the dummy straight out and send him. As he swims out, walk down the shore about 10 yards and wade out into the water a short distance. From there, encourage your dog to return straight to you, which requires an angled swim relative to the shoreline. But since you are in the water, he won't be tempted to go straight to the bank. You repeat this, walking back and forth between two points on shore about 10 yards apart, always wading out to receive your returning dog. This introduces him to angling toward you in water rather than heading straight for shore, and it does so without risk of failure.

Purpose of Drill

This drill teaches your dog to angle toward you rather than swim straight for shore in his water returns. It is a preliminary step for the Dobbs drill (below).

Prerequisites

Your dog should be steady and doing significant water singles. He should have learned to take straight lines through hazards on land. He should have been force-broken (to avoid delivery problems in water).

Equipment and Facilities

You need only one dummy, preferably a highly visible large white one.

You need a pond with two adjacent shorelines that are reasonably straight and joined by a reasonably square corner. The water should be open (no obstacles) swimming water, with a little wading water near shore.

Precautions and Pitfalls

Don't overwork your dog in any one session.

Process—Steps in Training

Set up on one end of the pond, about 10 yards from the corner. Toss the dummy about 10 yards straight out into the water. As your dog swims toward it, you should run around the corner and position yourself on the side of the pond about 10 yards from the corner. When your dog gets the dummy, encourage him to return straight to you. Since no angle is involved, and since you are about as far away as you would have been had you not moved, he will come straight to you. Good! Praise him!

Now toss the dummy back where it fell last time and send him again. This time run around the corner of the pond back to the place where you threw the first dummy. Again encourage him to return straight to you. As with the first retrieve, he will do it because it is no more difficult than returning to where you were when you threw the dummy. Repeat this a couple more times, running back and forth around the corner of the pond. This process, ridiculously simple as it may be, conditions your dog to return to you, even after you move to a new location. It breaks the habit of always returning to the place from which he was sent.

Next, stand on the long side of the pond, toss the dummy straight out about 10 yards, and send your dog. As he goes out, walk down the shore, away from the corner, about 10 yards, and wade out knee-deep into the pond (so your dog can touch bottom when he reaches you). When he gets the dummy, encourage him to return directly to you. Since you are in the water, he will see no point in returning to land. He will come straight to you, which involves angling into the shoreline. Repeat this drill a few times, walking back and forth between two points about 10 yards apart, to condition him to angle toward you when you are standing in shallow water.

With this preparation, your dog should go through the Dobbs drill with minimal corrections.

Addenda

If possible, repeat this drill in several locations before going into the Dobbs drill. You won't eliminate the corrections in the latter—nor should you want to, for they are necessary to "convince" your dog—but you will minimize them.

Dobbs Water Return Drill

Jim Dobbs invented this trial-and-error drill, which uses the e-collar's hot-spotting ability to teach young retrievers to return straight to the handler even when that means angling into shore rather than swimming straight to it. In this drill, you toss a big white dummy straight out into a pond a short distance and send your dog. As he goes out, you walk down the shoreline about 10 yards. When he gets the dummy, you encourage him to swim straight to you. To do so, he must angle in. If he refuses and swims straight back to the spot from which you tossed the dummy, let him get there, then nick him there with the e-collar to create a hot-spot. Then you repeat the entire drill from your new location. After a few corrections, he will angle toward you rather than swim straight back to where you were when you tossed the dummy. Finally, when you are close enough to one end of the pond, you toss the dummy straight, and as your dog goes out, you run to the end of the lake and encourage your dog to swim straight to you. This will mean that he must swim parallel to the shore for a long distance.

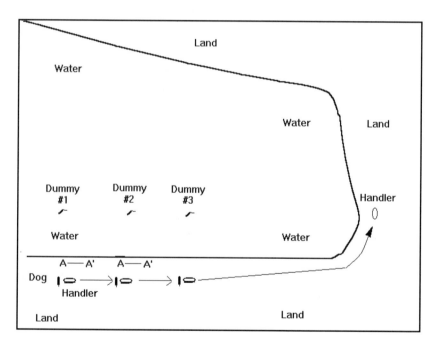

Figure 10. Dobbs Water Return Drill.

Purpose of Drill

This drill teaches angled returns in water, and is an excellent preparation for the drills that teach angling into and out of the water on the way to the dummy.

Prerequisites

Your dog should be steadied and doing significant water singles. Ideally, he should have been through the above "Drill to Introduce Straight Water Returns." He should have been force-broken and collar-conditioned.

Equipment and Facilities

You need just one dummy, preferably a highly visible big white one. You need an e-collar, preferably with momentary stimulation. For the final stages of this drill, you need good legs and lungs, for you will have to sprint some distance to the end of the pond.

You need a pond or lake, free of snags and hazards, one with a reasonably straight shoreline at least 60 yards long, with swimming water close to shore all along it, and you.

Precautions and Pitfalls

The e-collar correction should be a single, quick nick, not a sustained zapping.

Avoid overworking your dog in any one session.

Process—Steps in Training

With your dog sitting at heel, toss a big white dummy straight out about 10 yards into the pond. Send your dog. As he goes out, walk down the shore about 10 yards. After he gets the dummy, encourage him to return straight to you. If, instead, he swims to the nearest spot on shore (where you were when you threw the dummy), let him reach shore. Then nick him with the e-collar. This will create a hot-spot at that location. Now, walk toward your dog and have him deliver as near as possible to where he landed. Quickly toss the dummy back into the water and send him. Then walk 10 yards down shore again. When he gets the dummy, encourage him to swim straight to you. This time, he will almost certainly avoid the hot-spot, but he may cut into shore between there and where you are standing [anywhere between A and A' ("A-Prime") in the diagram]. If he does, when he reaches shore, nick him with the e-collar, thereby creating another hot-spot. Walk toward him, take the dummy, toss it out, and send him again. Walk down the shore again. When he gets the dummy, encourage him to swim straight to you. This time, in avoiding the two hot-spots, he will probably come straight to you. Great! Praise him! (If he again cuts into shore, repeat the above process. Eventually, he'll do it right.)

Because the retrieves are only 10 yards, he shouldn't be too tired to continue. Toss the dummy straight out again and send him. This time walk down shore about 10 yards, and encourage him to return straight to you. If he cuts into shore too soon (between A and A' in the diagram), correct him as above. When he will swim straight to you when you are 10 yards down the shore, repeat the drill a few more times, to more fully condition him.

Finally, toss the dummy out one more time, but this time run to the end of the pond, which should be at least 20 or 30 yards away, and encourage him to swim straight to you. After the preliminary work, he will almost certainly do it right the first time. If not, you know how to deal with it.

Addenda

Although a trial-and-error drill, this one starts your dog out in angles in the water very gently.

Angle-In Drill

This is primarily a trial-and-error drill, with a brief trial-and-success introduction. It has been around, in one form or another, as long as we've had American retriever field trials. Before the e-collar, most trainers used "correction techniques" we no longer mention in polite society . . . so I won't mention them. Suffice it to say that the modern e-collar has elevated this drill from, say, an "R" rating to at least a "PG."

In this drill, you use the e-collar's hot-spotting technique to teach your dog to take an angle into the water on his way to a mark, even when he sees an obvious and inviting path around the water on land. Hot-spotting makes the end-run less attractive than the angled-entry route straight toward the fall.

Purpose of Drill

As the name states, this drill introduces the dog to take angled entries into water when going for a retrieve.

Prerequisites

The dog should have completed the Dobbs drills for angled returns before starting this drill. He should have been force-broken and collar-conditioned.

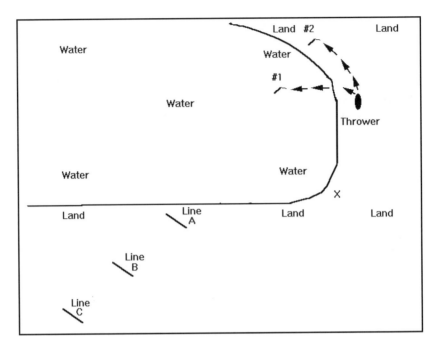

Figure 11. Angle-In Drill.

Equipment and Facilities

You need an assistant. A dummy launcher won't do because of the different angles of throw required, especially in the initial stages of this drill. You need several highly visible large white dummies. You are using this drill to teach angles, not marking, so after your dog takes the angle, he should have no difficulty finding the dummy. Big white dummies will draw him like a magnet.

You need an e-collar, preferably with momentary stimulation.

You need a pond with a corner that offers a clear path around it on land. The water should be open swimming water, and the land should not have much cover. On the side where you set up the line, you need fairly flat land for 30 to 40 yards, so you can move the line back as you progress through this drill. You should set the test up with a "square" (not angled) exit near the fall. That way, after your dog takes the angle into the water, everything else is straightforward for him. You should teach angled exits separately (see the "Angle-Out Drill").

Precautions and Pitfalls

The e-collar correction should be a single, quick nick, not a sustained zap.

Keep the swim short, so you can rerun your dog several times without overworking him in any one session.

Process—Steps in Training

Set the drill up as shown in the diagram. Start out at line A, the one closest to the water. Your assistant should toss the first dummy into the water (position #1 in the diagram). Since the dummy is in the water and the line is so close to the shore, your dog will jump in and swim to the dummy. Actually, you run this first retrieve just to "pattern" him into the water—to teach him that going by water brings correction-free success.

Next, your assistant should throw the dummy on land (position #2 in the diagram). After swimming for the first dummy, your dog may well swim for this one, too. If he does, great! But if he runs the bank, let him go. Say nothing. When he reaches position X, lightly nick him with the collar. That's all. Continue saying nothing. Let him get the dummy and return to you. If he returns by land (whether or not he swam going out), nick him at or near position X. After he delivers, have your assistant throw another dummy to position #1 (in the water), and send your dog for it. This will reinforce the notion that the water route is more pleasant than the land route. Next rerun with the dummy thrown to position #2 (on land).

After he goes by water both ways from line A for a dummy at position #2, move back to line B. Your assistant should throw the dummy to position #2 (on land). If your dog runs the bank, nick him at position X, if possible both going and returning. Then have your assistant throw the dummy to position #1 (in water)—to show your dog the correct route again.

After he goes by water both ways from line B for a dummy at position #2, move back to line C and repeat the process. Stay at each line until he does the drill correctly, that is, until he goes by water both ways when the dummy is thrown to position #2.

Addenda

You won't condition him fully in one training session, or in one location. Repeat this drill regularly, and if possible, change locations each session. Use different ponds, or at least different locations of the same pond.

To keep his spirits up, end each session with a simple water mark in which he will not be tempted to run the bank. If nothing else, give him two or three "fun dummies" in water just before you take him home.

Angle-Out Drill

This is primarily a trial-and-error drill, with a brief trial-and-success introduction. It is almost a mirror-image of the Angle-In Drill (above). Here the entry is square (not angled), but the exit near the fall is angled. Your dog will enter properly, but will be tempted to cut into the bank before getting all the way to where the dummy fell. If he succumbs to that temptation, you use the e-collar's hot-spotting ability to convince him that such "cheating" is a very bad idea indeed.

This is another drill whose rating went up from "R" to at least "PG" because of the modern e-collar.

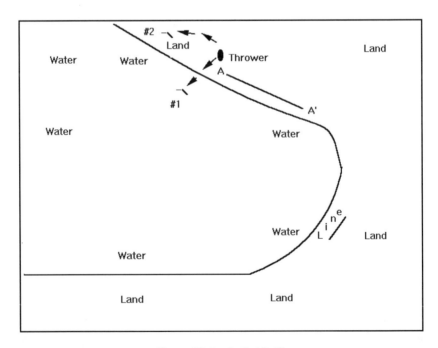

Figure 12. Angle-Out Drill.

Purpose of Drill

This drill teaches another piece of "honesty" in water. Specifically, it teaches the dog to continue swimming straight at a fall rather than detouring into land to run the bank.

Prerequisites

Your dog should have been through the angled return drills before starting this one. He should have been force-broken and collar-conditioned.

Equipment and Facilities

You need an assistant. A dummy launcher won't do because of the different angles of throw required, especially in the initial stages of this drill. You need several highly visible large white dummies. You are using this drill to teach angles, not marking, so after your dog takes the angle, he should have no difficulty finding the dummy. Big white dummies will draw him like a magnet.

You need an e-collar, preferably with momentary stimulation.

You need a pond configured so you can set the line up where it will give your dog a square entry and an angled exit. The land around the fall should be reasonably flat bare ground (or very light cover), so your dog will find the dummy easily.

Precautions and Pitfalls

The e-collar correction should be a single, quick nick, not a sustained zap.

Keep the swim short, so you can rerun your dog several times without overworking him in any one session.

Process—Steps in Training

Set the test up according to the diagram, with the line near the water's edge. Your thrower should first toss a dummy to position #1 (in the water). This is to pattern your dog to swim at an angle to the far shore as he goes toward a visible dummy in the water. Next, your thrower should toss a dummy to position #2 (on land). This time, your dog will probably cut into shore and land somewhere between points A and A'. Say nothing. Let him land. But, as soon as he does, nick him with the e-collar. If, on the return, he runs the bank, nick him about every 10 yards all the way back. If, at any point, he jumps in and swims, or even wades, stop nicking him. You want to hot-spot the land, not the water.

If you had to nick him going or coming, your thrower should next toss a dummy to position #1 (in water), to again pattern your dog to swim straight at it. Follow that with another toss to position #2 (on land). If he cheats (lands too soon), nick him again. If he runs the bank on the return, nick him repeatedly again.

If you had to nick him going or coming, rerun the entire test: first a toss to position #1 (in water) to pattern him, followed by a toss to position #2 (on land) to test him.

When he finally does take the correct line, praise him with great exuberance as he picks up the dummy. Then, if he's not too tired, run him a couple more times to condition him more fully to take this angle.

Addenda

You won't condition him fully in one training session, or in one location. Repeat this drill regularly, and if possible, change locations each session. Use different ponds, or at least different locations of the same pond.

To keep his spirits up, end each session with a simple water mark in which he will not be tempted to run the bank. If nothing else, give him two or three "fun dummies" in water just before you take him home.

Points and Islands Drill

This trial-and-error drill teaches your dog that last element of "honesty" in the water. A totally "honest" dog swims straight to and from the fall. He takes angled entries. He takes angled exits. And, finally, he doesn't detour to inviting pieces of land *en route*.

This drill uses the e-collar's hot-spotting ability to teach the dog not to detour *en route*, going or coming. In it, you run your dog on a simple single mark across water with an island or point just off-line somewhere between the line and the fall. When he yields to temptation and lands on the island or point—as he will at first—you correct him with the e-collar. This makes that piece of land a hot-spot, a place he will avoid in the future. Of course, you must repeat this drill many times in many places before your dog will be fully conditioned.

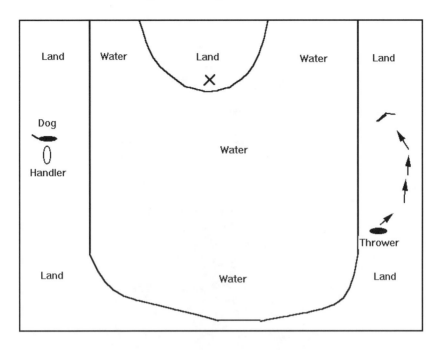

Figure 13. Points and Islands Drill.

Purpose of Drill

This drill conditions your dog to ignore points and islands lying just off his path to and from single marks in water.

Prerequisites

Your dog should have completed his angled entry and exit drills. He should have been force-broken and collar-conditioned.

Equipment and Facilities

You need an assistant or a multi-shot dummy launcher. You need several dummies, preferably highly visible large white dummies. You need an e-collar, preferably with momentary stimulation.

You need a pond with a point or an island that enables you to set this drill up properly

Precautions and Pitfalls

The e-collar correction should be a single, quick nick, not a sustained zap.

Don't set the test up with the path from the line to the fall too close to the point or island. Initially, set it up with the point or island a significant distance off-line, so your dog must detour badly to reach it. If he does indeed "cheat" this way, the magnitude of his detour will help him understand why he is being corrected. If you were to set it up with the point or island close to the line he should take, he might think you nicked him for leaving your side, in which case he would no-go next time. Later, after he understands what you want, you can snug the hazard up at least somewhat closer to his intended line. But, even then, set it up so the path to the fall is clearly separated from the point or island.

Keep the marks as short as your ponds allow. You want to teach the concept, not test your dog's endurance. And, of course, even with short marks, don't overwork your dog in any one session.

Process—Steps in Training

Set the drill up according to the diagram. Signal for a throw, and when the dummy lands, send your dog. If he detours to that inviting piece of land, great! Just what you want! Say nothing and do nothing, until he has all four feet on land. Then nick him with the collar. Let him continue on and make the retrieve. If he detours coming back (whether he did going out or not) nick him after he lands. If you had to nick him going or coming, immediately rerun the test. If he detours again, nick him again.

Whenever possible, run this test three times in a location: first, to get the correction in; second, to see that it took; and third, to further condition your dog in "doin' good." Of course, eventually, when he takes the correct line the first time, without detouring, skip the reruns—in fact, celebrate, for you're making progress.

Addenda

If possible, change locations each session, and use as many locations as you can find. To keep your dog's attitude up, mix in other types of work in which he doesn't get into trouble. It also helps to end each session in which you have nicked him with a couple of "fun dummies" in the water.

7
Double Mark Concepts
and
Preliminary Drills

CONCEPTS

A double marked retrieve (a.k.a. "double mark" or more simply "double") is a marked retrieve involving the falls of two birds. As stated before, a "marked retrieve" is one in which the dog sees the birds fall, as opposed to a "blind retrieve" in which he doesn't. In a double mark, each bird falls in a different and distinct location, so that each "area of the fall" is separated from the other. The dog should "mark" and remember each fall and, on command, retrieve them one at a time.

To mark them, he must remain steady until both birds are down. If he breaks immediately for the first bird, he probably won't see the other one fall. Even if he happens to see it as he races toward the first bird down, he will almost certainly turn the test into a circus, running back and forth between the two, perhaps finding neither.

Natural Sequence of Retrieves

Since the second bird down is fresher in his mind, a dog instinctively retrieves that bird first, and then retrieves the first bird down last. Call it "biblical sequence." *The last shall be first and the first shall be*

Opposite: Mike Gallagher and his Flat-Coated Retriever, "Scandal" (Harmony's Black Sox Scandal MH UDX OA WCX HoF), demonstrate good between-bird line manners. Scandal is returning with the go-bird. Mike has already turned to face the memory bird. When Scandal sits to deliver, he will be facing his next retrieve.

99

last. Because of this natural sequence of retrieves, we call the first bird down the "memory bird," since the dog must remember it while retrieving the other bird. For many decades, we called the second bird down the "diversion bird." But then, with the advent of hunt tests in the early 1980s, the term "diversion bird" came to have another meaning. Hunt-test judges frequently set up tests in which an "extra" bird is thrown as the dog returns with another bird. Unfortunately, this extra bird became known as a "diversion bird," which created considerable confusion. So, some ingenious soul invented the term "go-bird" for the last bird down in any multiple marked retrieve, whether double, triple, quad, or whatever. Why "go-bird"? After that bird is down, the handler sends his dog, so it's the bird on which the dog goes. In this book, to avoid confusion, I will call the last bird down in a multiple mark the "go-bird," reserving the term "diversion bird" for an extra bird thrown as the dog returns.

Switching

In a double mark, the dog should retrieve the two birds one at a time, without switching. A dog can switch in two ways: First, he can drop one bird to go after the other; second, he can give up hunting for one to hunt for the other. The dog that does either substantially reduces the likelihood that he will complete both retrieves. He also disturbs cover between the two birds unnecessarily. Thus, switching is a major no-no in retriever circles. Chapter 9 offers more detailed information on what constitutes a switch and how to prevent them.

Line Manners in Dog-Games

As stated before, in dog-games, the term "line manners" covers everything both the dog and handler do while at the line. In a double mark, the handler's job is to help his dog mark and remember both falls. Obviously, a dog can best mark a bird when he is sitting facing it when it falls. Therefore, in a double, both the handler and the dog should initially face the memory bird. Then, after it's down, they should shift around to face the go-bird. (The "chronic breaker," discussed below, is an exception.) This shifting at the line not only facilitates better marking of each bird, but it aligns the dog properly for his first retrieve, the go-bird. In dog-games, the dog must remain steady until the judge indicates he can be sent, typically by "calling his number." Thereafter, the handler may send his dog anytime. He need not send him immediately, and indeed he should not do so if his dog has glanced away from the go-bird. Instead, he should encourage the dog to re-focus on the go-bird—by shifting around, patting his leg, or whatever. Only when the dog is again properly focussed should he send him.

As the dog returns with the go-bird, the handler should turn to face the memory bird. That way, when the dog sits at heel to deliver, he'll be properly aligned for his next retrieve. The handler should take the go-bird and put it out of the dog's sight (typically behind his, the handler's, back, on the side opposite of the dog). The handler should then give his dog time to remember and re-focus on the memory bird. Only after the dog "locks in" on it should the handler send him. After the dog departs, the handler should give the go-bird to one of the judges.

When the dog returns with the memory bird, the handler should take it, give it to the judge, say "Thank you," and heel his dog away from the line.

The Chronic Breaker

Any retriever that is birdy enough to bother with will break occasionally. However, some retrievers are worse about it than others, and a few are almost incorrigible. If you have one of this last type of critters your number-one priority at the line is keeping him steady until the judge calls your number. Thus, you'll find that shifting to face each fall, as described above, does more harm than good. The more your dog moves around at the line, the more apt he is to break. Consequently, you should bring him to the line, plant him in the optimal compromise position, and insist that he remain there until you send him. In most double marks, you put your dog in the optimal position when you set him up facing about halfway between the two falls, thereby giving him equal visibility of both. Fortunately, most chronic breakers are outstanding markers, so this compromise position won't adversely affect such a dog's marking.

Suggestions for Improving Line Manners

If your dog is not a chronic breaker, you can help his marking considerably by training him to shift around with you between falls, as described above. You should start this during basic obedience training, long before you start double marks. That way, when you do start them, your dog will already know how to shift around with you at the line.

Start training him to shift as soon as he knows how to heel and sit automatically when you stop. With him sitting at heel, shift around about 45 degrees, without taking a step. As you do, command *Heel*, and encourage him (with the lead and chain training collar) to follow you. First teach him to shift to the left, so you can turn into him, and bump him with your knee as you do. After he has mastered that—so well that he moves before you bump him—teach him to shift to the right, when you move away from him. Use little jerk-and-release corrections with the lead to induce him to move around with you. After he has mastered the 45-degree turn in both directions, make your turns larger and smaller. Shift sometimes just a little bit, sometimes a lot, and occasionally turn in a half-circle (180 degrees). Always insist that your dog realign himself to face the direction you are facing.

Some trainers use two commands: *Heel* for left turns; *Here* for right turns. Do so if you please, but *Heel* will work for both. However,

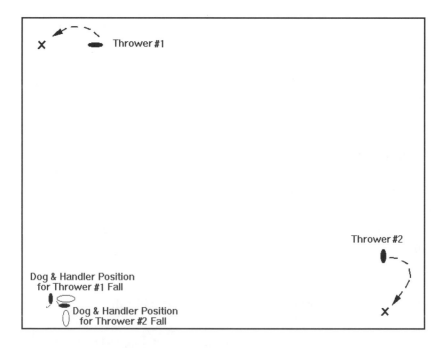

Figure 14. Shifting to Face Each Fall.

you should drop any and all commands after your dog understands this little exercise. When you are doing a double mark in a dog-game, you cannot say anything to your dog. So, early on, he should learn to shift with you without a command. If, from the time you begin double marks in training, you form the habit of remaining silent at the line, you'll be less apt to blurt out *Heel*, or whatever, while under judgment.

(*Nota bene*: In hunt tests, you will sometimes be asked to point a shotgun at each bird while it's in the air. If you teach your dog to look in the direction in which you are pointing your gun, which is explained later in this chapter, he will more easily turn with you in such tests.)

After your dog shifts with you automatically in basic obedience, you're ready to handle him that way in the introductory "Barrier Doubles" drill (below). Use the belt cord to control him. Sit him initially facing the memory bird. After it's down, shift around to face the go-bird before signaling for it. If necessary, guide him around with you with the belt cord. That's all there is to it, at least for double marks. (Triples add significant complications.) With time, your dog will shift with you, even off-lead, so automatically that neither you nor he will be conscious of it.

A few years ago, while I was out with a pointing breed training group, I ran Flick, my English Springer Spaniel, on a very simple triple mark—just to show these folks what other kinds of dogs can do. After watching Flick shift with me between falls, without breaking, one guy said, "My golly! My kids never minded that well!"

"Neither did mine!" I answered.

Left Hand?

Many give their dogs a left-hand signal along with the verbal command to retrieve. I expressed my objections to this, except for chronic breakers, in Chapter 2. However, I must make a slight modification for double marks. On both birds of a double, your dog will perform better if you keep your mitt out of his peripheral vision, *as long as he is locked in solidly on the area of the fall*. However, whenever he is not properly locked in, you should help him recall and focus on the fall by using body English to bring him into proper alignment, and then by placing your left hand beside his head. You might even say "Good!" softly to confirm his focus. You should do this in two situations: first, if, before you send him for the go-bird, your dog swings his head back and forth between the two falls; second, if, when you set him up for the memory bird, he seems uncertain about where it might be.

But, otherwise—whenever he is solidly locked in, and clearly in control of the situation—just send him with the voice command. Why distract him with your hand?

Adapting Line Manners to Hunting

After your dog shifts automatically with you this way, you can easily extend this skill to various hunting situations, like when you are sitting on a stool, or even in a boat. You can easily extend this training so that your dog learns to look in the direction in which you are pointing your shotgun, as explained later in this chapter.

PRELIMINARY DRILLS

Before getting into the actual double-mark training drills in Chapters 8 through 10, we should go through a couple of preliminary drills: the "Barrier Doubles," with which you introduce your dog to the concept of a double mark in a totally positive manner; and the "Marking off the Gun Barrel" drill, with which you teach your dog to look for birds in whatever direction you point your shotgun.

Barrier Doubles

This bare-ground trial-and-success drill introduces your dog to the concept of double marks. It lets him form good habits without corrections. By using the belt cord, you can induce your dog to shift with you at the line and you can keep him from breaking. The barrier between the two falls prevents him from switching. Since you are running on bare ground, he can't fail to find each fall in turn. Thus, he forms initial habits of waiting for both falls to go down, of shifting with you between the falls, of retrieving the two dummies one at a time, without switching. After enough work in this barrier drill, your retriever will be conditioned to do doubles correctly, at least as far as trial-and-success techniques can do that. Thereafter, with sundry trial-and-error techniques, you must teach him the folly of the various errors he will later be tempted to make.

In the diagram, the barrier that prevents the dog from switching is a fence. However, it can be anything that will block his path from one dummy to the other: a wall, a body of water, a line of vehicles, a tennis court, a building, or whatever. If you use a tennis court or building, the line should be at one corner, with the two marks down adjacent sides.

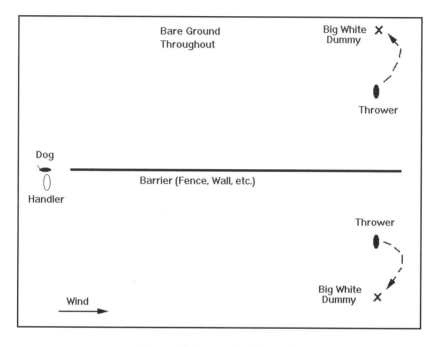

Figure 15. Barrier Doubles Drill.

Purpose of Drill

This drill teaches initial good habits in double marks: steadiness, shifting between falls, retrieving the dummies one at a time, and not switching. You should start your dog into double marks with this drill and stay with it until he has formed all of these good habits reasonably well.

Prerequisites

The dog should be obedience-trained, force-broken, steadied, and doing significant single marks. He should have learned to shift with you as described above.

Equipment and Facilities

Initially you can throw both marks yourself. However, to facilitate your own handling at the line, you really need two assistants to throw for you, or two multiple-shot dummy launchers. Single-shot dummy launchers would be inadequate because reloading them after every double mark would disrupt the flow of the training.

You need several dummies, preferably the highly visible large white ones. You also need your belt cord.

You need a suitable bare-ground area, one with a barrier that prevents switching.

Precautions and Pitfalls

Don't override your dog's natural ("biblical") retrieving sequence. In fact, insist that he retrieve the go-bird first, then the memory bird. Much later, after he is doing significant doubles in cover, you may want to teach him to "select" (as explained in Chapter 13), but not now.

Don't slip into the habit of having either the left or the right fall thrown first all the time. Mix them up, left-right, right-left.

Don't disdain the belt cord, no matter how steady your dog may be.

When he is returning with the first dummy, don't let him elude you and go after the second dummy. Initially with Beaver (Chesapeake), I played linebacker and he played fullback. Several times I had to tackle him and roll in the dirt with him to keep him from getting past me.

Don't overwork your dog in any one session.

Process—Steps in Training

Set the drill up according to the diagram, on bare ground with a "dog-proof" barrier between the two falls. Bring your dog to the line *on the belt cord* and set him up facing the memory bird. All through his initial work on doubles, he should be on the belt cord. You can use it not only to guide him so he shifts with you between falls but also to prevent him from breaking. No matter how steady he is on singles, he will be strongly inclined to break when that second bird of a double appears. With the belt cord, you can prevent a breaking habit from starting.

Signal for the memory bird. After it's down, let your dog stare at it a couple of seconds (to form a good marking habit). Now, shift around to face the go-bird, guiding your dog with the belt cord if necessary (as it probably will be). Signal for the go-bird. After it's down, make him wait briefly before you send him. If he swings his head back around toward the memory bird, use the belt cord to bring him back to the go-bird. Never (never, never) send him when he's looking the wrong way. When he's properly locked in on the go-bird, send him. While he is returning, turn so you are facing the memory bird. That way, when he sits at heel to deliver, he'll be facing his next retrieve. Encourage him to come in and sit at heel before delivering. Grip his collar with your left hand (to keep him steady) and take the dummy with your right hand. Hold the dummy behind your right hip. When your dog locks in solidly on the memory bird, send him.

Rerun the test, but reverse the order of the falls. Go back and forth like that a few times, but not so often that your dog gets tired or bored.

Addenda

Change location as often as you can, but always use bare ground (so your dog will find both dummies). Use the four corners of your house, the four outside corners of a tennis court, a school-yard fence with an opening for the walkway, and so on. Stay with this drill until you are sure your dog understands the concept, namely that he is to retrieve the two falls one at a time, that he must deliver the first one before going after the second.

Marking off the Gun Barrel

This trial-and-success drill teaches your dog to look for birds in whatever direction you point your shotgun. In both hunting and hunt tests, this facilitates seeing, and therefore marking, the falls. If your dog hunts with you long enough, he will eventually pick this up on his own. However, you can "shorten his learning curve" substantially with this simple little drill. In it, position two assistants with dummies a short distance from the line, with plenty of space between them. These two assistants take turns tossing dummies for your dog. You point your shotgun at each dummy while it's in the air. As it reaches the high point of its arc, the assistant who threw it fires a blank pistol to attract your dog's attention. Back and forth you go, from one assistant to the other. Enough repetitions of this drill will condition your dog to look in whichever direction you point your shotgun, even before your assistant shoots his blank pistol.

Purpose of Drill

This drill conditions your retriever to mark off your gun barrel. This helps him see and therefore mark falls both in hunting and in hunt tests.

Mary Jo Gallagher and Fortune demonstrate how to teach a dog to mark off the gun barrel. Here Mary Jo points toward the thrower on the left . . .

. . . and here she points toward the thrower on the right.

Prerequisites

Your dog should be steady on single marks. He should know how to shift with you at the line, as described above.

Equipment and Facilities

You need two assistants, each with a blank pistol and several dummies, preferably highly visible large white ones. You could also use two multi-shot dummy launchers. You need a shotgun or, better yet, a reasonable facsimile thereof. You need a suitable bare-ground area.

Precautions and Pitfalls

If you use a real shotgun rather than a facsimile, make sure it is empty. Even though you won't be pointing directly at your assistants, you will be pointing it in their general directions. Accidents do happen. Frankly, you would be better off to saw a shotgun facsimile from an old piece of wood and paint it to resemble a shotgun.

Keep the retrieves short and on bare ground. You are teaching your dog to mark off your gun barrel, so he should have no difficulty finding the dummies.

Don't overwork your dog in any one session.

Process—Steps in Training

Position your two assistants about 25 yards from the line in plain sight, with an angle of 90 to 120 degrees between them. You and your dog should face halfway between them. Initially, you should squat down by your dog (or sit on a stool) to make your shotgun more visible to him.

Signal for a throw from either assistant. As the dummy goes up, shift around toward it and point your shotgun at it. As the dummy reaches the top of its arc, your assistant should shoot his blank pistol to attract your dog's attention. When the dummy lands, send your dog. Repeat the process with the other assistant. And so on, back and forth several times in each session. After a few such sessions, your dog will look for a dummy in whichever direction you point your shotgun, even before he hears the shot.

Then, stand up and repeat the drill. Initially, you might lean forward a little as you point the gun, so your dog can more easily see where you are pointing it.

Next, have your assistants hide behind trees, bushes, or whatever. Signal for a throw from either one and point your shotgun at the dummy as it appears. Again, as the dummy reaches the top of its arc, your assistant should shoot his blank pistol to attract your dog's attention. Repeat this with the other assistant. Then go back and forth a few times, to cement the concept in your dog's mind.

Repeat this entire drill fairly often, and in many different places and situations. Eventually, your dog will mark off your gun barrel almost as naturally as he retrieves the birds you shoot.

Flatcoat Black, Ch. windfall's Flatland Fortune, SH, WCX.
Owner: Mary Jo Gallagher.

Addenda

This drill and the line manners shifting between falls described above work well together, reinforcing one another nicely. Both build teamwork between you and your retriever, whether in hunting or at the line in a hunt test.

8
Double Mark
Memory Drills

This chapter presents two drills for improving your retriever's marking and memory in doubles: "Memory Bird Rehearsal," and "Reruns." It also presents a drill for introducing your dog to two types of tests used in dog-games, namely, "Retiring Gun" and "Hidden Gun" tests.

Another technique, "Salting," which is covered in Chapter 5, can be useful in doubles, especially for the memory bird. If, when starting doubles in cover, you salt the area of the fall for the memory bird, your dog has a much better chance of succeeding without assistance.

DRILLS

Memory Bird Rehearsals

You can help your dog remember the memory bird in a double mark by "rehearsing" it as a single immediately before running the double. This trial-and-success technique is highly useful when you first move into cover. Then, later on, whenever you introduce your dog to a new and especially challenging double, you should help him out by rehearsing the memory bird as a single before asking him to do the complete double.

Purpose of Drill

This drill has two purposes, one obvious, the other subtle. Obviously, rehearsing the memory bird as a single will help your dog remember it when he runs the complete double. Like all reruns, it lets him see the fall a second time when he knows exactly where it is coming down. Thus, the rehearsal both "calibrates his marking eye" for that fall and helps him remember it better.

More subtly, it builds his self-confidence. He will almost certainly succeed on the double after rehearsing the memory bird. If you rehearse frequently while he is learning basic doubles, and then again whenever you introduce a new concept, your dog will not doubt his ability to find both birds. If an inexperienced dog fails too often on his initial doubles, or even on new doubles later on, he will lose confidence in himself. Many such dogs, convinced that they will fail, begin to no-go. In fact, any time your dog no-go's a double, you should first suspect that he lacks confidence, and rehearse the memory bird before running the complete double.

Prerequisites

Your dog should be ready to move into cover for double marks.

Equipment and Facilities

You need only whatever you are using for the intended double.

Precautions and Pitfalls

As in reruns (below), your memory bird assistant should throw the dummy to the same spot in both the rehearsal and the regular run. If he throws it to two different places, the rehearsal will do more harm than good. Similarly, if your assistant must help your dog out during the rehearsal, he should do it as described in *Dealing with Loose Hunts in Training* in Chapter 2.

You should neither over- nor under-do this drill. When first starting doubles in cover, use it regularly, at least until you feel your dog no longer needs it. When you stop rehearsing the memory bird, you might, as a precaution, "salt" the memory bird area the first few times you run him on doubles "cold turkey." Later on, whenever introducing your dog to a new doubles concept, you should first decide whether he needs a rehearsal, whether he needs just salting, and whether he can take on the new challenge unaided by either technique. Only you can know your dog that well.

When your dog is doing good work on reasonably difficult doubles and shows signs of adequate self-confidence, you should stop both rehearsing and salting. Don't overwork your dog in any one session.

Process—Steps in Training

Set up an appropriate double for your dog. Then, before running him on the complete double, run just the memory bird as a single. If he has much difficulty with it as a single, you should consider whether this particular test is beyond his current abilities. If you decide the test is okay for him, rehearse the memory bird again before running the entire test. You will accomplish nothing positive by throwing a double at him before he can handle the memory bird as a single.

Addenda

Rehearsing takes less time than rerunning an entire test, so use it in preference to the rerun during all of your dog's introductory work, that is, during both his initial doubles in cover and during his introduction to each new concept in doubles.

Reruns

You should use this highly effective trial-and-success technique all through your dog's active life. In it, you simply rerun any test with which he has difficulty on his initial run. In fact, if he still has difficulty with it on the rerun, you should rerun him again, as long as he isn't too tired.

Purpose of Drill

Reruns improve the dog's marking, memory, and confidence. In the rerun, the dog sees each fall again from the line, after finding out exactly where each one is coming down. He remembers the falls better the second time. Because he remembers them so well, and because he knows exactly where they are, he feels quite confident that he can find them.

Prerequisites

As soon as you introduce your dog to doubles in cover, you can (and should) start rerunning him on all tests he doesn't do quite well the first time.

Equipment and Facilities

Since the rerun should be an exact repetition of the initial test, you need exactly what you needed for the initial run, no more, no less.

Precautions and Pitfalls

To make reruns effective, your assistants must throw the dummies so they fall in the same places every time. Scattering them here, there, and everywhere will confuse, not help, your dog. The effectiveness of the rerun depends on it being an exact duplicate of the initial run. This, of course, means that, if your assistant has to help your dog out on the initial run (or any subsequent run), he should do it as described in *Dealing with Loose Hunts in Training* in Chapter 2.

Don't overwork your dog in any one session.

Process—Steps in Training

If, on a double mark, you are not satisfied with your dog's work, immediately rerun him on the same test. But how should you decide when to be satisfied? If he pins both falls, you should be ecstatic! If he finds both after relatively short and tight area-hunts, grin and put him up. If he goes into a somewhat "loose hunt" before finding the dummy on either fall, rerun him. And, of course, if he has to be helped on either fall, rerun him. If in doubt, let other circumstances make the call. Is your frustration indicator banging on "overload"? Is your dog tired? Is it getting late? Have your training buddies had fair shares of time to train their dogs in this session?

Addenda

Generally, you should rerun the entire test exactly as you ran it initially. However, sometimes you can save a little time by shortening up the go-bird. If your dog pinned the go-bird but had trouble with the memory bird, do this on the rerun: Have the memory bird thrown exactly as it was initially thrown; but, then, instead of having the go-bird repeated, simply toss a dummy off to the side from the line as a substitute for the go-bird. That will divert your dog's attention from the memory bird adequately for the rerun, and it will reduce the time the rerun takes, especially if the original go-bird was long or in water. Little shortcuts like this make more time available for everyone in the training group.

In recent years, a few prominent pros have begun "evangelizing" against reruns. In Chapter 5, under the "Reruns" drill, you'll find explanations of what their arguments are, of what could be motivating this strange development, and of why their arguments against reruns are not relevant for amateurs training their own dogs.

Introducing Retiring Guns and Hidden Guns

Dog-game judges frequently use "retiring guns" or "hidden guns" to test the participating retrievers' marking and memory. Retiring gun tests occur in both field trials and hunting tests, but more frequently in the former. Hidden gun tests occur exclusively in hunting tests because visible guns are a requirement in field trials.

In a retiring gun double mark, both sets of guns start out standing in plain sight, so the dog can see them from the line. However, after the memory bird guns throw their bird, they move behind some convenient obstacle (bushes, trees, whatever) where they cannot be seen from the line. Thus, when the dog returns with the go-bird and sets up for the memory bird, he can no longer see the guns out there. If he has "marked off the guns," he's in big trouble. From the dog's perspective, this test approximates rather closely the visual situation in a double mark in actual duck hunting. The dog sees the flock come in, perhaps watches it circle, and sees a bird fall from it. Then he is distracted by another bird falling somewhere else. He retrieves this second bird first. When set up for the first bird, he no longer has the flock as a visual aid.

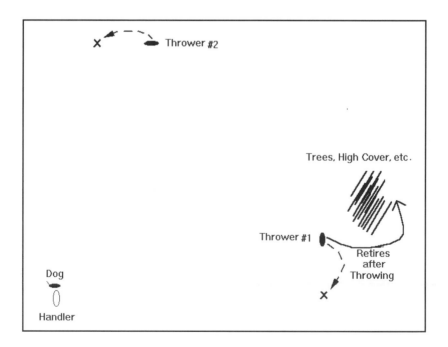

Figure 16. Retiring Gun Test.

Because it so resembles the dog's visibility in actual hunting, the retiring gun test should be a popular test in hunt tests. However, because it has been so long identified with field trials, and because a certain animosity exists between participants in the two games, the retiring gun test has taken on something of a bad name in hunt test circles. Too bad.

In a hidden gun double mark, both sets of guns are hidden before the dog and handler approach the line. The dog never sees them. Before throwing their birds, each set of guns makes some sound—usually a shot or a few squawks on a duck or pheasant call—to attract the dog's attention. Then, after throwing the bird, they shoot as the bird reaches the high point of its arc. The dog must mark both falls without the using gunners as visual aids. This simulates dove hunting, or even duck hunting when singles are flying here and there. Most hunt-test double marks are of this type. (Sometimes, one set of guns is hidden and the other set is standing in plain sight.)

Retiring gun and hidden gun tests are treated together here because you use the same drill to introduce your dog to either of them. That trial-and-success drill is based on reruns. You first run the double

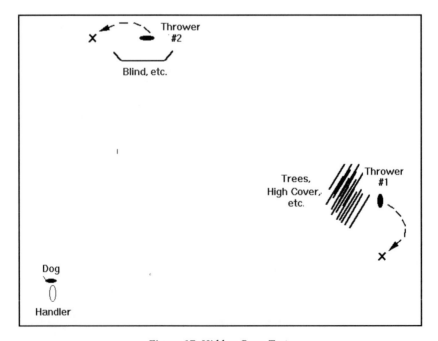

Figure 17. Hidden Guns Test.

with both sets of guns in plain sight throughout. Then, on the rerun, you change the test to either a retiring gun or hidden gun test.

Purpose of Drill

This drill will ease your dog into either retiring gun or hidden gun tests with a minimum risk of failure.

Prerequisites

Your retriever should be doing fairly challenging doubles with both guns in plain sight before you introduce either retiring or hidden guns.

Equipment and Facilities

You need two assistants with blank pistols and several dummies. You need a field or lake with natural or artificial places of concealment for the throwers.

Precautions and Pitfalls

Don't rush your dog into or through this phase of training. Although you can start retiring or hiding the throwers *on reruns only* earlier in your dog's doubles work, you should resolutely resist the temptation to throw these gimmicks at him on initial runs before he's ready. If you're the impetuous type, forget it until your dog is quite far along in doubles.

Don't overwork your dog in any one session.

Process—Steps in Training

Set up an appropriate double mark. Run the test with both sets of guns remaining visible throughout. To save time, instead of running the entire test, you might simply rehearse the memory bird. Either way, if your dog has too much trouble, repeat the initial run before proceeding.

Next, rerun the same test, but change it into either a retiring gun or hidden gun test. For a retiring gun test, have your memory bird guns retire *after your dog turns to watch the go-bird fall.* For a hidden gun test, have both sets of guns totally hidden on the rerun.

Repeat this technique in many doubles in many locations before you first run your dog on such a test "cold," that is, without the initial run with the guns in sight. Use your own judgment of your dog's readiness to guide you here. If he wobbles too much on his first "cold" test, go back to running initially with both sets of guns in place.

Addenda

Both tests are excellent simulations of hunting. If you are a hunter, you should give your dog plenty of them after he is ready for them. Introduce him to both concepts and then mix them up in your regular training.

9
Double Mark Switch-Proofing Drills

As indicated in Chapter 7, a dog can switch in two ways: "bird-to-bird," in which he dog drops one bird to pick up or go after another; and "area-to-area," in which he abandons the area of one fall to go to the area of another fall. The bird-to-bird switch is straightforward, altogether without subtlety. However, over the years, retrieverites who participate in dog-games have refined the definition of the area-to-area switch, almost *ad nauseam*.

The best current thinking on the area-to-area switch specifies that a dog switches in this way only when he goes to the area of one fall, establishes a hunt, leaves that area, and goes to the area of another un-retrieved fall. This definition contains two subtleties: First, the dog must "establish a hunt"; second, he must go to the area of another fall that contains a bird. To establish a hunt in the initial area, the dog must go there, put on the brakes at least a little, and begin to search for the bird. If he simply runs through the area, he has not switched, at least not technically. Further, if he establishes a hunt in one area, then leaves and returns to the area of an "old fall" (from which he has already retrieved the bird), he has not switched, again at least not technically. To switch then, the retriever must go to the area of one fall, establish a hunt there, then leave that area and go to the area of another un-retrieved fall.

Please keep in mind that these are *human* definitions, developed over the years by dog-game participants for reasons that shall soon be apparent to you. You should know them, especially if you plan to participate in these sports. However, don't expect your dog to master such hair-splitting distinctions! If, in training, you correct him only for a "proper" switch, but let him get away with whatever falls outside of this nicely refined definition—namely, running through an area without establishing a hunt, and returning to old falls—your dog won't understand the difference. Consequently, you'll never fully switch-proof him. So, in training, whenever he leaves the area of one fall, with or without establishing a hunt, and goes to the area of another fall, with or without a bird in it, you should treat it as a switch, and correct him appropriately.

Then, why bother with these nit-picky distinctions? Elementary, my dear Watson! You must know them under three sets of circumstances. First, if someday you run your retriever in dog-games, they'll help you engage the judges in meaningful dialogue when you disagree with their decision to drop your dog for switching. (Hint: If your dog actually switched, you should argue that he hadn't *really* established a hunt in the first area; or, if he returned to an old fall, you should point out that, no-way no-how, is that switching, and that your dog shouldn't be penalized as if it were.) Second, if someday you become a dog-game judge, these same nit-picky distinctions will help you defend yourself against the protests of participants who engage you in meaningful dialogue about your decision to drop their dogs for switching. (Hint: To end the discussion quickly—whether the dog actually switched, but the handler claims he hadn't established a hunt, or the dog returned to an old fall—you should explain that you dropped the dog for disturbing too much cover unnecessarily, rather than for switching.) Third, if someday you write a book covering multiple marked retrieves, you *dasn't* omit this hair-splitting explanation of what is and what isn't switching, lest you outrage dog-game participants and judges. Otherwise, these legalistic distinctions serve no purpose.

But, clearly, to merit so much attention from so many clever human minds for so many years, switching must be a very big deal. Indeed, it is. In dog-games, it's a hanging offense. A dog that switches—in either a field trial or a hunting test—is *ipso facto* immediately dropped.

Why? For three reasons. First and most importantly, the dog that switches will seldom retrieve both birds, at least without being handled. Often, a dog not trained in handling will fail to find either bird. He may repeatedly run back and forth between the two areas—as may the dog that runs through an area without establishing a hunt and the dog that returns to an old fall. Second, a switching dog disturbs cover unnecessarily between the falls—as does the dog that runs through an area without establishing a hunt and the dog that returns to an old fall. Finally, the dog that switches shows a lack of perseverance—as does the dog that runs through an area without establishing a hunt and the dog that returns to an old fall.

For these reasons, area-to-area switching is a very serious fault (and so are the related faults of running through an area without establishing a hunt and returning to old falls). Happily, dogs don't understand the difference between the three crimes, so you can cure all three with the same techniques. This chapter contains three drills to help you accomplish that. The "Basic Switch Correction" allows you to cure all three area-to-area problems, that is, switching, running through an area without establishing a hunt, and returning to old falls. The "Dirt Clod Switch-Proofing" drill facilitates systematic curing of area-to-area switching and returning to old falls. The "Bulldog" enables you to cure the bird-to-bird switch.

DRILLS

Basic Switch Correction

This trial-and-error training technique addresses all three forms of area-to-area mistakes (switching, running through an area without establishing a hunt, and returning to an old fall). It becomes a drill through the number of random repetitions it takes to switch-proof the average retriever. In it, you do nothing unusual to induce a dog to err, other than gradually tighten up the marks. Mostly, you wait for your dog to slip up naturally, as most young dogs are all too wont to do. Whenever he does, you let him go all the way to the area to which he is switching. When he does, you should correct him right there. This creates a hot-spot, a place to which he will be reluctant to return. Then, you immediately rerun the entire test.

Purpose of Drill

This technique, repeated as opportunities arise in normal training on double marks, gradually cures your dog of area-to-area switching, running through areas without establishing a hunt, and returning to old falls.

Prerequisites

Your dog should be doing widespread double marks in cover. (And,

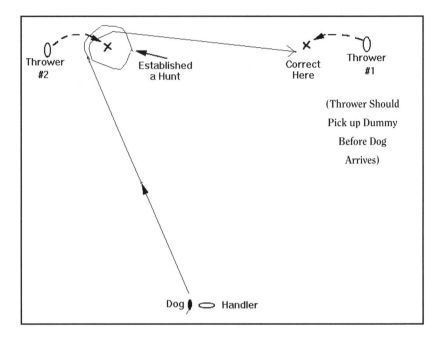

Figure 18. Basic Correction for Switching.

of course, he must be making one of the three mistakes in normal training when you employ this technique.)

If you plan to correct him with the e-collar, he should have been
collar-conditioned.

Equipment and Facilities

You need only what you are using in normal training when your
dog switches, runs through an area without establishing a hunt, or
returns to an old fall.

If you intend to correct him electronically, you need an e-collar,
preferably with continuous stimulation. If you don't intend to use the e-
collar, you need good legs and lungs, to run out and correct him personally, and eventually to run him down when he sees you coming and
knows that you have unfriendly intentions.

Precautions and Pitfalls

Over-correction is a great risk here. If you overdo it very often,
your dog may start blinking (avoiding) the area of the fall. Or he could
develop a no-go problem.

Process—Steps in Training

You can't use this technique until your dog gives you an opportunity. Of course, you shouldn't be the least picky about whether he is fulfilling the complete definition of a switch. Any time he leaves the area of one fall and goes to the area of the other—whether or not he has established a hunt in the first, and whether or not there is still a bird in the second—correct him as directed here.

When he leaves one area and heads for the other, say nothing and do nothing until he reaches the second area. (To prevent him from getting the dummy there, the thrower should pick it up before your dog arrives.) When your dog reaches the area of that fall, correct him. If you use the e-collar, zap him. Then have the other thrower, the one in the area your dog left when he switched, help him out (as described in Chapter 2, under *Dealing with Loose Hunts in Training*.)

If you don't use the e-collar, you should run out to your dog and correct him personally in the area to which he has switched. If, as you run toward him, he takes off to get away from the correction he knows is coming (as he will after a few experiences), run him down silently. Don't call him to you. Don't stop him with the whistle. Simply catch him. (I did this often when I was young, but now I let my fingers do the running.) When you get your hands on him, say nothing, do nothing to him. Just grab him by the collar and drag him back to the area to which he switched. Drag him; don't heel him. Were you to give him any command before getting back to the area to which he switched (where you will correct him), he would think you were correcting him for obeying whatever command you gave him. Thus, give no commands as you run him down, no commands as you "transport" him back to the area in which you want to correct him. When you get him there, correct him appropriately. Give him the evil eye, shake him lightly, give him a stroke with a whip, or do whatever you and he have worked out as appropriate punishment. Then heel him to the other area, show him the dummy, have him pick it up, and leave him there, holding the dummy, in a *Sit-Stay*. Walk back to the line and call him in to you. When he arrives, praise him! (He has now done it correctly and needs the reassurance, especially after the recent correction.)

Then rerun the entire test. If, on the rerun, your dog picks up both marks without switching, you corrected him about right. If he repeats the switch, you didn't correct him firmly enough. If he refuses to go to the hot-spot area even to make a normal retrieve, you have over-corrected him (in which case you should move to another location before proceeding). This is one of the few situations in retriever training when your dog tells you immediately whether you applied the right amount of correction.

Since the correction is necessarily rather mild, your dog won't remember the first one very long. Eventually, he will switch again. So you should be prepared to correct him this way again. And again. And again. Gradually, he will figure out that bad things happen every time he switches, runs through an area without establishing a hunt, or returns to an old fall. So he will stop committing these canine felonies. Success, at last.

Addenda

Some e-collar trainers, after zapping the dog, handle him back to the correct bird. That works, but I prefer to minimize handling on marks, lest the dog grow too fond of the idea and begin to pop. So I recommend having the thrower help the dog out.

Dirt Clod Switch-Proofing

Using the "Basic Switch Correction" (above) whenever the opportunity arises, you can eventually cure your dog of area-to-area switching, running through an area without establishing a hunt, and returning to old falls. However, you may want to put a little more control, a little more system, into the process. Perhaps you are blessed with a dog that marks so magnificently well that he almost never switches. (I've seen a few, but never owned one.) Perhaps you need to speed the process up to get your dog ready for a rapidly approaching test or trial. Perhaps you have already switch-proofed your dog, but want to give him a little brush-up work. Or perhaps you're just too damned impatient to wait for random switches. (I fall in this last category. My wife says I must still have all the patience I was born with, since I haven't used any of it yet. I like to think that I'm saving it, so I won't run out later on.)

Whatever your reason, if you want to systematize and hasten the process, this trial-and-error "Dirt Clod" drill was made for you. It will induce your dog to switch or return to an old fall when and where you want him to. (It cannot induce him to run through an area without

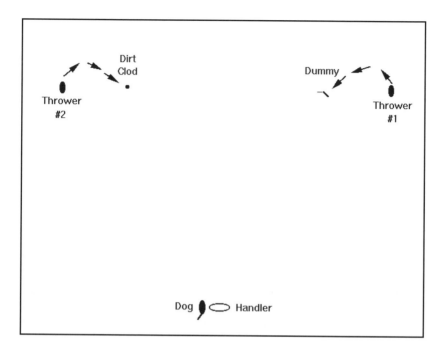

Figure 19. Dirt Clod Switch-Proofing.

establishing a hunt.) In this drill, you substitute a dirt clod for the dummy at one station in a double. From the line, it looks like a dummy or bird. Naturally, your dog won't find anything when he hunts that area . . . so, sooner or later, he will switch. When he does, you can correct him.

Purpose of Drill

This drill allows you to trick your unschooled retriever into perpetrating either of two area-to-area mistakes (switching or returning to an old fall) when and where you want. This facilitates curing him in a timely and organized way.

Prerequisites

Your dog should be doing widespread doubles in cover. If you plan to use the e-collar, he should have been collar-conditioned.

Equipment and Facilities

You need two assistants with blank pistols and several dummies.

Since both throwers have active "human" parts, dummy launchers won't suffice. You need several dirt clods about the size of a pigeon. If you live in a rocky area, you can use rocks instead of dirt clods.

If you plan to correct your dog electronically, you need an e-collar, preferably with continuous stimulation. If you don't plan to use the e-collar, you need good legs and lungs, so you can run your dog down and correct him.

You can use whatever fields you normally use for double mark training.

Precautions and Pitfalls

Don't overdo this drill by using it training session after training session without mixing in a few good days. Since it allows you to induce switches at will, you may be tempted to concentrate exclusively on switch-proofing until you've finished it. But that many consecutive days of corrections, corrections, and more corrections can discourage your dog. If he gets into trouble every training session, he will develop an negative attitude. (Wouldn't you?) To prevent that, mix in plenty of "happy" sessions, in which he does everything right.

Don't overwork your dog in any one session.

Process—Steps in Training

Set up a double appropriate for your dog. But one assistant should throw a dirt clod instead of a dummy. If the go-bird assistant throws the clod, you are setting your dog up to switch. If the memory bird assistant throws it, you are setting your dog up to return to an old fall. Work it both ways.

When your dog gives up in the area with the dirt clod and heads for the other area, let him go all the way there. Then correct him as described in the "Basic Switch Correction." While you are doing that, the thrower who used the dirt clod should surreptitiously slip a dummy into the area of his fall. Then you can proceed exactly as you would do in the "Basic Switch Correction."

After your dog has been through this "Dirt Clod" drill enough times, he will neither switch nor return to old falls. Thereafter, in this drill, after hunting in the dirt clod area for a reasonable length of time, he may do any of three things, all bad: He may give up and return to you; or he may continue to hunt there, but without enthusiasm; or he may wander off somewhere other than the area of the other fall. Don't give him time do any of these things. Before he reaches that point, have the throw-er slip a dummy into the dirt clod area while your dog isn't looking. That way he will find it and feel successful. Incidentally, when your dog reach-es this point, he is well switch-proofed, so you can discontinue this drill.

Addenda

Initially, tricking your dog with this drill may prick your con-science. However, after you see how much it speeds up the process (and how forgiving your dog is), your twinge of guilt will disappear. After all, you're curing an undesirable natural tendency. Were it not for this nat-ural tendency, you wouldn't be able to trick him into switching.

"Bulldog" (Diversion Bird)

This trial-and-error drill cures your dog of bird-to-bird switching. If you plan to run him in hunt tests, you should use this drill to prepare him for "Bulldog" tests, in which, as your dog returns with a bird (nor-mally the go-bird), an "extra" set of guns pops up and throws a bird (the

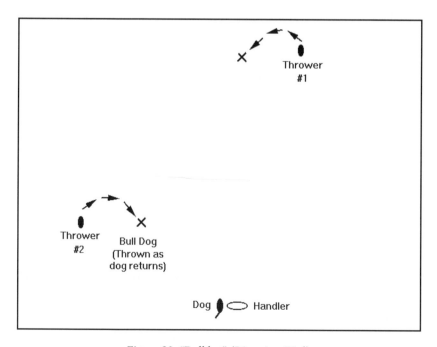

Figure 20. "Bulldog" (Diversion Bird).

"Bulldog"). This bird may be thrown anywhere, but the closer it is to your dog's path as he returns to you, the more it will tempt him to switch. In this drill, you start out with the Bulldog quite a ways from his path. Then you gradually "snug" it up until it falls immediately in front of him.

In hunt tests, as in hunting, your dog is expected to retrieve the Bulldog after he delivers the bird he was carrying when the Bulldog was thrown.

Purpose of Drill

This drill cures the dog of bird-to-bird switching.

Prerequisites

Your dog should be force-broken before you start this work, so he understands what *Fetch!* means. Beyond that, there really aren't any prerequisites. You can start this drill while your dog is still doing only single marks.

Equipment and Facilities

You need two assistants with blank pistols and several dummies. Or you could use one dummy launcher (for the go-bird) and one assistant (for the Bulldog). You can use any type of field, even bare ground to start out with.

Precautions and Pitfalls

Your dog may have difficulty finding the Bulldog bird when sent to retrieve it. He saw it from one location, and you send him for it from another, so he hasn't had a fair chance to mark this bird. If he can't find it and wanders around out of the area of the fall, don't get upset with him. Simply have the thrower help him, or handle him to it.

Process—Steps in Training

Start out running just a single mark and a Bulldog. Set the test up with the Bulldog 180 degrees from the single, that is, straight behind you as your dog approaches you with the go-bird. That way, you can prevent a switch—physically if necessary. Make the single quite simple and, if possible, have the Bulldog fall where it will be in plain sight from a distance. You're curing a type of switch, not extending his marking ability. Run the single and, as your dog returns to you, signal for the Bulldog. If he heads for it, as he almost surely will at first, block him from getting past you. If he eludes you, your assistant should quickly pick up the Bulldog, to prevent him from "succeeding."

(*Nota bene*: As the Bulldog goes up, some trainers blow the *Sit*-whistle. Then after it's down, they blow the *Come-in* whistle. This is an excellent technique, one which leads eventually to having the dog sit and watch the Bulldog, perhaps without a whistle. Such a dog gets a much better look at the Bulldog than does the moving dog.)

If your dog dropped the go-bird as he headed for the Bulldog, heel him back to the dropped bird, and command *Fetch!* Leave him sitting there while you walk back to the line. Now whistle him in. When he arrives, praise him (to better identify the "safe" place in such a test). If he tried to break for the Bulldog, don't send him to retrieve it. Instead, rerun the entire test. If he does it properly (doesn't break for the Bulldog, doesn't drop his bird, and does return to you with it), send him for the Bulldog.

When he can handle this 180-degree Bulldog, begin to reduce the angle. As you do, you lose more and more of your ability to block his path if he switches, so don't rush. As in so many training situations, a short success is better than a long failure. Whenever your dog begins to switch when you can't block him, do as follows: Have your assistant pick up the Bulldog before your dog can get it; run at your dog, catch him, drag him back to the bird he abandoned, and go through the *Fetch!* . . . *Sit!* . . . *Come!* routine again. Unless you are young, athletic, and in good shape, keep these Bulldogs short and near you, so you don't have to run so far.

Eventually, you'll be able to have the Bulldog dropped right in front of him without incident. At first, have it dropped a long way ahead of him, in fact, right in front of you, so you can get to it before he does. Then, gradually have it thrown in his path farther and farther from you. Work at this regularly and your dog will learn to deal properly with Bulldogs wherever they may fall.

Addenda

Bulldogs occur in water as well as on land, but you should do your initial training on land—even though he will be less tempted to switch in water, because of the difficulty of the medium itself. On land, he can handle more repetitions without tiring. And, on land, you can get to him when you need to.

10
Double Mark
Head-Swinging

Most retrievers, while learning double marks, slip into the counterproductive and aggravating habit of "head-swinging." This fault can take two forms, either of which adversely affects the dog's marking and memory. In the first type, as soon as the memory bird comes down—sometimes even while it's still falling—the dog swings his head around to look for the go-bird. This happens most frequently when the memory bird is a control bird and the go-bird is a shot flier. In dog-games, if the guns are visible from the line, a retriever can tell when one station is about to shoot a flier, which is far more exciting than a control bird. Dogs learn to distinguish between the two because three people (one thrower and two shooters with shotguns) normally stand at a flier station, whereas only two (one thrower and one popper with a blank pistol) normally stand at a control bird station. Knowing this, a dog may swing around from the ho-hum control bird to the exciting flier before he has had an adequate opportunity to mark the former. Consequently, he frequently pins the go-bird, but has all sorts of difficulty finding the memory bird.

In a dog-game, about the only defense against this type of head-swinging is to stand so you block your dog's view of the go-bird station until after the memory bird is down. Some handlers try to keep their dogs from so much as seeing the flier station until then. However, that increases the risk of a break when the flier surprises the dog. So other handlers allow their dogs to see the flier station, but then block it until the memory bird is down. To do this consistently, a person must train his dog to work from either side. That way if the flier is on the right, he can work his dog from his left side, which puts him on the dog's right side. Similarly, if the flier is on the left, he can work his dog from his right side, which puts him on his dog's left side.

As stated above, that is about the only defense against this type of head-swinging when it happens at a dog-game. However, by using the drill described below in training, you can prevent it from happening.

In the second type of head-swinging, the dog watches the memory bird well, and swings around to see the go-bird at the proper time, but, before being sent, he looks back around at the memory bird. Then he may even swing his head back and forth several times between the two falls, which can only weaken his marks on both birds. Or he may remain locked in on the memory bird, which dims his memory of the go-bird.

If the handler sends him when he is looking at the memory bird, the dog can make any of three serious mistakes. First, he might go to the memory bird area, establish a hunt, then quickly switch to the go-bird area. Second, he might run through the memory bird area without establishing a hunt and head for the go-bird, thereby disturbing cover between the falls unnecessarily. Third, even if he finds the go-bird satis-factorily, he might, when sent for the memory bird, wonder whether he hasn't already picked it up, since he started in that direction before retrieving the go-bird. Thus, he might head straight for the go-bird area again, which is returning to an old fall. But let's say he avoids all three serious mistakes. Let's say that, when sent initially, he does indeed com-plete the retrieve of the memory bird first. Let's even say that he does a better job on it than he would have done had he retrieved the birds in the normal sequence. His mark on the go-bird bird will be weaker than it should be, so his gain on the memory bird is washed out by his loss on the go-bird.

Consequently, whether in a dog-game or in training, if your dog swings his head back to the memory bird after the go-bird is down, you shouldn't send him until you bring his head (and mind) back to the go-bird. If you send him when he's looking the wrong way, you can gain noth-ing, and you risk three serious errors. How should you bring his head back around to the go-bird? If it's to the right of the memory bird (and your dog is on your left), turn away from him and pat your leg to bring him around. If the go-bird is to the left of the memory bird, turn into and slightly in front of your dog to force him to turn toward the go-bird.

So much for how to deal with both types of head-swinging after the fact. How can you prevent these habits from getting started? Well, you can take a giant step in that direction by training your dog to shift with you as you turn to face each mark just before the bird is thrown, as described in Chapter 7. If, instead, you set your dog up in one position at the line and keep him there through both falls, you encourage head-swinging. But if, after the memory bird is down, your dog shifts around with you to face the go-bird station, he will be less inclined to swing his head back to the memory bird after the go-bird is down.

But what if your dog is a chronic breaker? Chapter 7 explains that, since shifting between falls encourages such dogs to break, anyone who has one should plant him in one position for both falls. Happily, chronic breakers normally aren't head-swingers. They lock in so tightly on the most recent bird that you might have difficulty physically bending their heads around to another fall, previous or forthcoming.

If your dog is not a chronic breaker, you should train him to shift with you between falls. He'll almost certainly still swing his head occasionally, but it won't become a habit as easily, and the drill described below will be more effective in curing any head-swinging problems he develops.

DRILLS

"Stop Counting!" Drill

This drill teaches the dog that he cannot rely on his own eyes to tell him how many falls he is about to see. When you bring him to the line, he sees two throwers standing out there in plain sight. Your dog's experience to-date tells him he is about to run a double mark. But you fool him. You run each fall as a single, using the other as a decoy, so to speak. Back and forth you go like this. Then you sneak in a double. Then back to singles. If you do this often enough, he will lose faith in his own ability to predict how many falls he will see in a given test. This will encourage him to pay attention only to the bird in the air, and ignore extra gunners out in the field.

Purpose of Drill

This drill helps the dog stay focussed on each fall as it is thrown for him, rather than to look immediately for another. It also helps him remain focussed on each fall, rather than peek back at the previous fall. In other words, it cures, at least temporarily, both types of head-swinging.

Prerequisites

The only prerequisite is that your dog has begun to swing his head in either of the two above-described ways on double marks.

Equipment and Facilities

You need two assistants with blank pistols, or two dummy launchers, or one assistant and one dummy launcher. You also need several dummies.

You need a suitable field, typically with light to moderate cover and no hazards. You should not make the marks difficult, for you want your dog to succeed easily on each retrieve.

Precautions and Pitfalls

Don't overwork your dog in any one session.

Process—Steps in Training

Set up a relatively simple double mark for your dog. Both assistants should be visible from the line. If you use dummy launchers, each one should be marked somehow (perhaps with a chair) so your dog can spot them from the line.

Heel your dog to the line and let him look at both stations. Then set him up in your normal manner. Signal for either bird. After it's down, send your dog for it. When he returns with it, set him up again and signal for the other bird. When it's down, send him. Go back and forth like this a couple of times. Then, give him both falls as a double. Finally, give him each fall as a single again. That's the total procedure when everything goes right, which it seldom will, at least at first. Now let's look at how you operate when things don't go right, that is, when he swings his head during this drill.

If he swings his head toward the other station after a single mark is down, help him re-focus on the single that is down before you send him. If you send him while he's looking the wrong way—in "See! Serves ya right!" mode—he will learn nothing. He'll wobble out toward the wrong assistant, and wander all over the pasture. Instead, make sure he's looking at the mark that was actually thrown before you send him. Then, immediately rerun the same mark. If he swings his head again, repeat the above, and then rerun the same mark again. Do that mark as a single until he doesn't swing his head two successive times. Then go to the other mark, and repeat this process. When he has succeeded twice on it, too, give him the double.

If, when you intend to give him the double, he swings his head too quickly from the memory bird to the (anticipated) go-bird, don't signal for the go-bird. Instead, re-focus him on the memory bird and send him for it as a single. Repeat the memory bird as a single until he doesn't swing his head two successive times. Then try the double again.

If, on the double, after both birds are down, he swings his head back to the memory bird, immediately heel him off-line and have your assistants pick up the birds. In other words, give him nuttin'. When you bring him back to the line, give him the go-bird as a single until he doesn't swing his head two successive time. Then, try the double again.

Addenda

If your dog has learned to identify flier stations in dog-games, and consequently does the first type of head-swinging, set up such a double in training. Put three people, two with shotguns, at the flier station. Put either one or two persons at the control bird station. Then run the control bird as a single—again and again and again, until your dog stops swinging around to the flier station before you have shifted around to face the flier. This is a good drill to give such a dog shortly before a test or trial.

11
Triple Mark Concepts and Preliminary Drill

CONCEPTS

A triple marked retrieve (a.k.a. "triple mark" or more simply "triple") is a marked retrieve involving the fall of three birds. As stated before, a "marked retrieve" is one in which the dog sees the birds fall, as opposed to a "blind retrieve"in which he doesn't. In a triple mark (as in all multiple marks), each bird falls in a different and distinct location, so that each "area of the fall" is separate from the others. The dog should "mark" and remember each fall and, on command, retrieve them one at a time. Obviously, to mark all three falls, the dog must be steady.

When your retriever is ready for triples, he is already an accomplished worker. He has been obedience-trained, force-broken, steadied, and has mastered substantial "lesser" marks, both single and double. He has been switch-proofed, and may have learned to take angles in water. Even with all this behind him, he needs some preliminary work on triples, mostly on line manners and bare-ground triples, before advancing into "real" triples in cover and water.

Sequence of Retrieves

In doubles, the natural sequence of retrieves is uncomplicated: The dog works in "biblical sequence," retrieving the last bird down (the go-bird) first, and the first bird down (the memory bird) last. But a triple has *two* memory birds (as well as a go-bird). Of course, the dog should retrieve the go-bird first, just as in doubles. But which of the two memory birds should be next? Normally, you should let your retriever take whichever one he wants next. The choice will vary from triple to triple and from dog to dog. So, how do you know which one your dog wants in any given triple? Elementary! If you watch him as he returns with the go-bird, you will notice that he glances at least once at one of the two remaining falls. That glance should tell you which bird he has in mind, and therefore which one you should send him for next. As he approaches you with the go-bird, you should turn to face the fall he has thusly "requested." That way, when he sits to deliver, he will be properly aligned for his next retrieve. In most triple marks, that's how you can best help your dog pick up all three birds cleanly.

Later on, after he has had extensive experience in triples, you may want to teach him to "select," that is, to allow you to select the sequence of his retrieves in an order different from that to which nature inclines him (see Chapter 13). But, initially, you should let him pick them up in the order he finds most comfortable.

Line Manners in Dog Games

As stated before, the term "line manners" covers everything that both the dog and the handler do while at the line. In all marking tests, the handler's primary job is to help his dog mark and remember the falls. Obviously, a dog can best mark a bird when he is sitting so he faces it as it falls. In triples, just as in doubles, unless your dog is a chronic breaker, you can best help him mark and remember the falls by training him to shift with you to face each fall immediately before it goes up. Set him up initially facing the first memory bird. After it's down, turn to face the second memory bird. After it's down, turn to face the go-bird.

The Chronic Breaker

If your dog is a chronic breaker, shifting around at the line between falls may tempt him to break beyond his strength to resist. Fortunately, as mentioned before, chronic breakers are usually excellent markers, so need less assistance at the line than most dogs. Set such a dog up in the best compromise position and keep him there until all three birds are down. The "best compromise position" depends on the sequence of the falls, and on how widely spread they are. If they are rather snug, you can usually get by with setting him up facing the middle bird. But, if they are extremely wide, like covering a total of 180 degrees with the go-bird as one of the outside birds, you may have to gamble on shifting him once just before the go-bird. To do that, you would set him up facing halfway between the two memory birds, and then after both of those are down, shift around to face the go-bird. Work all this out in training before you try it at a test or trial.

Suggestions for Improving Line Manners

As stated above, if your dog is not a chronic breaker, you should teach him to shift with you between falls. The location and sequence of the falls determines the appropriate "steps" for this man-and-dog "line-dance." In an "around the horn" triple—left-middle-right or right-middle-left—you simply turn twice in the same direction. However, any other sequence of falls (right-left-middle, left-right-middle, middle-right-left, or middle-left-right) you turn once in each direction. And the wider-spaced the falls the farther you must shift from one to another. To minimize really wide shifts, you may opt to set your dog up initially facing about halfway between the first and second fall and shift only once—to the go-bird after the first two birds are down. After you've been running triples with your dog awhile, you'll be able to figure out what line-manner technique helps him most in each situation.

Since, in your double mark work, you have already trained your dog to shift both ways with you, you won't have to teach him any new moves for triples. However, you will have to accustom him to shifting twice. Start in your backyard or in some bare-ground area. With your dog sitting at heel, toss three white dummies as a wide triple. Do this repeatedly to expose your dog to all six possible patterns: l-m-r, l-r-m, m-l-r, m-r-l, r-m-l, and r-l-m. This will not only accustom him to the different types of double shifts, but will introduce him, in a totally positive manner, to the various sequences in which triples can fall.

When you do this, wear a hunting or dog training vest to facilitate handling three dummies. Also use the belt cord, because your dog may break or at least creep when you throw the third bird, which he won't be expecting at first. Even a dog that is rock-steady on doubles may break on the unexpected third fall in a triple, at least at first. So be prepared.

In multiple marks, use your left hand only when your dog seems uncertain about his next retrieve. Mary Jo Gallagher demonstrates here with Fortune. Note also that she is holding the bird just delivered behind her on the side opposite her dog. Out of sight, out of mind.

Left Hand?

Should you help your dog out in triples by giving him a line with your left hand, much as you do in blind retrieves? Generally, you should not. Whenever your dog is locked in solidly on the proper fall, your hand can't possibly help him—but it may distract him from his mark. However, if he seems uncertain, if he doesn't lock in as he should, but perhaps glances this way and that, your left hand can be a life-saver for him. It will settle him down, give him a definite direction in which to look, even help him remember the fall. So, the general rule for all three birds of a triple is: Whenever your dog locks in properly, send him with just a voice command; however, if he seems confused, help him orient himself by putting your left hand by his head as if to give him a line.

Adapting Line Manners to Hunting

After accustoming your dog, in training, to shift with you between the falls on triples, as described above, you can easily adapt this skill to various hunting situations, like when you are sitting on a stool, or even in a boat. Since he undoubtedly already looks in the direction in which you point your shotgun, he should adjust to triples in hunting very naturally.

PRELIMINARY DRILL

Before getting into the actual triple-mark training drills in Chapters 12 and 13, we should go through one basic drill to introduce your dog to the triple mark concept on bare ground. This confidence-building drill will prevent your dog from developing a fear of failure when you move him into cover for triples.

Bare Ground Triples

You started doubles with the "Barrier Doubles" drill (Chapter 7) to keep your dog from switching while he developed self-confidence on bare ground. Then later you switch-proofed him. Switching should not be a problem when you start triples, but remembering three falls probably will be, at least at first. So you should again make everything quite simple for him while he develops self-confidence. To do this, start his triples on bare ground with big white dummies. He'll be able to see all three dummies from the line, so he won't develop any fear of failure as he learns this new "game" you've dreamed up for him. Were you to start in cover, he would fail often, lose confidence in himself, and, if you were to persist in such nonsense, he would start a nasty no-go habit. Then you would have to go back to bare ground to rebuild his confidence, and thereby spend more time than it takes to start him correctly in the first place.

By starting on bare ground with highly visible white dummies, you can extend the length of the falls very rapidly out to whatever maximum distance you have in mind. Since he will succeed every time, he will never develop a fear of long triples.

Purpose of Drill

This drill has two purposes: First, it conditions your dog to expect, to mark, and to remember three falls; second, it builds his confidence in his ability to do triples.

Prerequisites

Your dog should be doing challenging doubles, and should have been switch-proofed. He should have completed the above line manners preparations.

Equipment and Facilities

You need three assistants with a blank pistols and several large white dummies. Or you can use some mixture of dummy launchers and assistants. You need your belt cord (to control creeping and breaking on the third bird).

You need a bare-ground area large enough to allow you to set up the longest triple you intend to teach your dog.

Precautions and Pitfalls

Some bare-ground areas, especially those in town, have litter you should pick up before training your dog—food, broken bottles, and so forth. Since you will be using white dummies, make sure the area you use is cleared of white objects (plastic cups, napkins, and so forth) that could confuse your dog.

Keep the falls widespread, with at least 45 degrees between adjacent falls. With big white dummies on bare ground, tight marks might tempt your dog to switch. Don't overwork your dog in any one session.

Process—Steps in Training

Set up a widespread triple of a reasonable length. Set it up so all three falls are either downwind or in a crosswind. Upwind marks encourage quartering, which is not desirable in marked retrieves.

To assure success, first "rehearse" your dog on the two memory birds as a double. Then run the triple. As your dog returns with the go-bird, pay attention to him, so you can tell which of the memory birds he wants next. When he tells you (by glancing at it), turn to face that fall before he gets to you. That way, when he sits at heel to deliver, he will be facing his next retrieve. As he returns to you with the second dummy, turn to face the last remaining fall.

Repeat the triple, but change the sequence of the falls. In subsequent training sessions, vary both the sequence and the length of the falls. For a few sessions, "rehearse" the two memory birds as a double before running the triple, but discontinue this as soon as you feel he no longer needs it.

If possible, use several bare-ground areas for this training.

Addenda

When your dog is comfortable with long triples on bare ground, you should discontinue this drill and move into cover. When you do, shorten up and make the tests very simple. Even then, "rehearse" the two memory birds as a double (or as two singles) before running the triple.

12
Triple Mark Memory Drills

For memory work in triples, it's "something old, something new, something borrowed, something blue."

The Old? You should use the same two basic memory drills recommended in Chapter 8 for doubles, namely rehearsals and reruns. However, rehearsals have several additional dimensions in triples because the extra fall gives you an amazing number of choices relative to how much and which parts of the test to rehearse. These options are covered in the "Rehearsals" drill, below. Reruns are, of course, a staple in triples, just as in every phase of retriever training, as pointed out in Chapter 1, *"Repetitio est mater studiorum."*

The New? This chapter presents a new technique for stretching your dog's memory to the third bird in a triple: the "delayed triple." This turns a triple's normal two memory birds and a go-bird into two go-birds and a memory bird. That, of course, simplifies the test for the beginning retriever.

The Borrowed? You may at least occasionally be able to use the "salting" technique recommended in Chapter 5 for singles. However, salting has less application in triples, because of the dog's experience level. Usually, if such an advanced dog reaches the area of the fall, he finds the bird. He's less apt to wander off than he was when first starting out in doubles. Nevertheless, keep salting in mind, in case you need it.

The Blue? Beats me! But what analogy is perfect? Besides, three out of four jest ain't all that bad!

DRILLS

Rehearsals

In doubles, you have helped your dog mark and remember the memory bird by "rehearsing" it as a single immediately before running the complete double. This trial-and-success technique also works in triples. In fact, because of the additional memory bird, you have several additional options. First, you can run only the more difficult memory bird as a single. Second, you can run each memory bird as a single. Third, you can run the two together as a double thrown in the same sequence in which they will be thrown in the triple. Fourth, you can run them as a double with the sequence reversed. (Why would you want to do run them backwards? Well, if you are fairly certain that, in the triple, your dog will pick these two falls up in reverse order, you will help his memory a little more by running them that way in the preliminary double.) Fifth, if you're the entrenched belt-and-suspenders type, you can run each memory bird as a single, then run them together as a double before venturing into the triple. Sixth, if you're the belt-and-suspenders type with a flair for minor risk-taking, you can run only the more difficult memory bird as a single, then run the two memory birds as a double before trying the triple.

If you have a lively imagination, you can probably conjure up still more rehearsal options for triples. However, these six cover the practical situations—and, frankly, a couple that aren't so practical, too.

Purpose of Drill

You rehearse one or both of the memory birds of a triple for the same pair of reasons you rehearse the memory bird in a double (see Chapter 8): to help your dog mark and remember the rehearsed birds when you run him on the triple; and to build his self-confidence.

Prerequisites

Your dog should have completed his bare-ground work in triples.

Equipment and Facilities

You need three assistants with blank pistols and several dummies. Optionally, you can use some combination of assistants and dummy launchers.

You need a field or water appropriate for your dog's current capabilities.

Precautions and Pitfalls

As with all drills based on reruns, your assistants should throw the falls to the same spots every time. This includes those times when they must help your dog find the bird. (See *Dealing with Loose Hunts in Training* in Chapter 2 for instructions on how a thrower should help a dog find a mark.)

Don't overdo this drill. Use it when introducing your dog to triples in cover. As he gains experience and confidence, discontinue rehearsing and run him on basic triples "cold." Thereafter, whenever you introduce him to a new and challenging concept in triple marks, rehearse a few times before running him cold.

Don't overwork your dog in any one session.

Process—Steps in Training

As mentioned above, you have at least six options in rehearsing a triple. However, you should rely mostly on the following procedure, and fall back on the other options only as your own experience with your particular dog dictates.

Set up a triple of appropriate difficulty for your dog's current ability. Run the two memory birds as a double. If he has great difficulty with it, you should assess whether he is ready for this test yet. If you feel he is, run one or both of the memory birds as singles, then rerun the double. If all goes well, and he's not too tired, run the triple. That's about all there is to it.

As he gains experience and confidence, you can discontinue rehearsing both memory birds as a double. Instead rehearse only the more difficult of the two as a single. Then, when you feel your dog can handle it, start running him on triples of appropriate difficulty without any rehearsal.

Thereafter, all through his active life, whenever you introduce your dog to a new concept in triples, at least consider rehearsing one or both of the memory birds before running him on the triple.

Addenda

As mentioned in Chapter 8, rehearsing takes less time than rerunning the entire test, so use it as a time-saver, especially through your dog's introductory work on triples.

Reruns

In a "rerun," you run your dog again on a test, or some part of it, after he has completed the entire test (no matter how poorly) at least once. As with singles and doubles, reruns are the heart and soul of all trial-and-success memory drills for triples. This is just common sense, and is in complete compliance with what reputable animal behavior researchers (from Pavlov on) have advocated.

Purpose of Drill

Reruns improve the dog's marking and memory through the conditioning that results from rote repetition. As stated before, reruns "calibrate" the dog's marking eye, by giving him another look at falls from the line after he knows from experience precisely where each one is coming down.

Prerequisites

The only prerequisite for rerunning a triple is that, in the previous run of the same test, the dog has not covered himself with glory.

Equipment and Facilities

You need only what you used to run the original triple.

Precautions and Pitfalls

Don't bother rerunning tests your dog does well on his first run. But do rerun any test with which he has a significant problem.

In the rerun, your assistants (and/or dummy launchers) should throw the dummies so they land as near as possible to where they landed in the original triple. If a thrower must help your dog find a dummy, he should follow the instructions in *Dealing with Loose Hunts in Training* in Chapter 2.

Don't overwork your dog in any one session.

Process—Steps in Training

Whenever you are not satisfied with your dog's work on his initial run, rerun the test exactly the way you ran it the first time. The criteria for deciding whether you should be satisfied with his work are as follows. If he pins all three marks, you should be ecstatic! If he finds all three with short area hunts, grin and put him up. If he goes into a somewhat "loose hunt" before finding one or more of the falls, rerun him. And, of course, if he has to be helped on any of the falls, rerun him. If in doubt, let other circumstances make the call. Is your frustration indicator banging on "overload"? Is your dog tired? Is it getting late? Have all of your training buddies had their fair shares of time to train their dogs in this session?

If, after the rerun, you still aren't satisfied with your dog's work, rerun it again—assuming he's not too tired, there's still enough daylight, and your training buddies aren't getting hostile.

Addenda

Generally, you should rerun the entire test, exactly as you ran it the first time. However, you can often save time by rerunning only the fall or falls with which your dog had difficulty. If, for example, he aced the go-bird but had trouble with both memory birds, you should rerun both the memory birds, but instead of the go-bird you should simply toss a third dummy off the line in some "neutral" direction. If he did well on the go-bird and one memory bird and had difficulty with the other memory bird, you should rerun only the problem memory bird, tossing two dummies off the line in different "neutral" directions. Little shortcuts like this allow your dog to calibrate his eye on the troublesome fall without eating up too much training time.

In recent years, a few prominent pros have begun "evangelizing" against reruns. In Chapter 5, under the "Reruns" drill, you'll find an explanation of their arguments: what could be motivating them, and why their arguments against reruns are not relevant for amateurs training their own dogs.

Delayed Triples

This is an optional trial-and-success drill to ease an inexperienced dog into triples. In it, you set up a triple but have only two of the falls thrown. You send your dog for the go-bird. After he delivers it, you have the third bird thrown. It, of course, becomes a second go-bird, which your dog will retrieve next. After he delivers it, you send him for the memory bird from the original double.

This is not truly a triple mark because all three falls are never on the ground at once. It has two go-birds and one memory bird. It falls somewhere in the middle ground between doubles and triples.

Purpose of Drill

This drill accustoms an inexperienced dog to retrieving three birds in a single test, without requiring that he mark and remember all three at one time.

Prerequisites

You can begin this drill, if it appeals to you, as soon as your dog is doing reasonably challenging double marks.

Equipment and Facilities

You need three assistants with blank pistols and several dummies. Optionally, you can use some combination of assistants and dummy launchers.

You need a field or water appropriate for your dog's current capabilities.

Precautions and Pitfalls

This is simply an introductory drill. Don't stay with it too long, lest you waste time you could spend better in other drills.

Don't overwork your dog in any one session.

Process—Steps in Training

Set up a normal double for your dog and position your third assistant wherever you want the delayed mark to fall. Have the double thrown and send your dog for the go-bird. When he returns, after he delivers and is again sitting at heel beside you at the line, have the third bird thrown. Send him for that bird. When he returns, send him for the memory bird from the original double.

(If you want to take an added precaution, you can rehearse the memory bird of the double and then run the delayed triple as a rerun. However, if your dog is ready for this work, and if the marks are within his capabilities, he shouldn't need the rehearsal.)

After your dog has successfully completed the test as a delayed triple, rerun it as a regular triple, using the fall that was delayed as the go-bird. After running the delayed triple, your dog should have no difficulty with the same test run as a regular triple.

Addenda

Don't confuse this drill with the "diversion" test that is so common in hunting tests. In that test, the diversion (delayed bird) is thrown as the dog returns with the go-bird, not after he has delivered the go-bird and is sitting at the line. The diversion test is a switching tests, intended to trap the dog that hasn't been thoroughly switch-proofed into dropping the go-bird to go after the delayed diversion.

13
Selection

In a multiple marked retrieve—double, triple, quad, whatever—when a handler sends his dog for the falls "out of sequence," that is, in a sequence other than the one in which the dog would naturally retrieve them, the handler is said to be "selecting." From there, retriever jargon takes a curious twist, in that we say such a handler has trained his dog to "select," although the handler, not the dog, selects. Extending this linguistic *non sequitur*, we speak of a dog so trained as a "selection" dog, although, as noted, the handler makes the selections.

On any multiple mark, if the handler sends his dog first for a memory bird instead of the go-bird, he is said to be "primary-selecting," in that he is selecting the first (primary) bird the dog is to retrieve. If, for example, in a double, the handler, for whatever reason, sends his dog for the memory bird first, he is primary-selecting.

On any multiple mark with more than two falls, if the handler allows the dog to retrieve the go-bird first, but then sends him next for a memory bird the dog would not naturally retrieve next, he is "secondary-selecting." If, for example, in an "around-the-horn" triples (in which dogs normally retrieve the birds outside-outside-middle), the handler, for whatever reason, sends his dog for the middle bird second, he is secondary-selecting.

So much for terminology. The question immediately arises: Why would a handler override his dog's natural retrieving sequence? Good question, too. In fact, when you're at the line and have an inclination to select, you should ask yourself that very question: Why do I want to do this? If the answer comes back, "to wow the judges!" or "to dazzle the gallery!"—or anything else having nothing to do with improving your dog's performance—you should forget about selecting, at least in that particular situation. I mention this because so much of the selecting one sees at trials and tests seems to be intended to inflate the handler's ego rather than the dog's score. In fact, such show-boating often leads to a disaster in which the confused dog requires handling on one or more of the marks.

Nevertheless, selecting has a place, at least in dog-games. To understand that place, you must first realize that judges do not smile benevolently on "handling on a mark," that is, directing a dog to a mark with whistle and arm signals as in a blind retrieve. The judges set up blind retrieves to test the dog's responses to that sort of handling. They set up marks to test the dog's marking ability. When the handler has to handle his dog to a mark, the dog has failed that particular mark. Since, according to both common sense and all dog-game rules, "marking is of primary importance," failing a mark and therefore requiring handling is a serious fault. Thus, each handler should do everything he can to facilitate his dog's marking, that is, to improve the probability that he will pick up his marks without handling.

However, in some tests, a dog may be more apt to pick up the marks cleanly if he retrieves them out of the natural sequence. For example, in a triple, one memory bird may be significantly more difficult than the other (perhaps because of a retiring or hidden gun). In such a case, the handler may reasonably assume that his dog will be less likely to require handling on that difficult mark if he sends him for it second (after the go-bird), even though the dog would naturally choose the other memory bird. Thus, the handler would wisely secondary-select the more difficult memory bird. Another example: In a triple with the #1 fall very short and in the middle, the #2 fall long and to the left, and the go-bird long and to the right, the dog would naturally take them right-left-middle. But, in so doing, he would make two very long retrieves and then face a very short one. Many dogs overrun this short fall and must be handled back to it. Thus, a handler might reasonably conclude he can best get his dog through such a triple by primary-selecting the short #1 fall first, while it's fresh in the dog's mind. After picking it up, the dog faces only a wide double.

Clearly, occasions arise in which selection (both secondary and primary) make sense. But the only legitimate criterion for determining whether it makes sense in a given situation is: How will the dog be most apt to pick up all the marks without handling? If the answer is "with selection," selection is justified. If not, it isn't.

Of course, the individual dog's strengths and weaknesses must be pumped into this decision-making process. The better the dog's marking ability, the less often should his handler select his falls. (Hint to breeders: If you are looking for a stud to improve your line's marking ability, attend dog-games and look for dogs that pick up all their marks without selection and without handling.)

But, even if selection makes sense with your dog in a particular situation, you won't be able to pull it off unless you have first trained him to select. If you try it with a dog not so trained, you'll confuse him so much that you'll end up handling him more than you would have had you let him do it his way. In selection, and especially in primary-selection, you are going against the dog's natural inclinations. Thus, you must prepare him for the associated trauma. Of course, you shouldn't start such training until he has had plenty of experience in triple marks. (As indicated above, selection is possible on any multiple mark: double, triple, quad, and so forth. However, if you were to begin selecting in doubles before your dog is well along in triples, and especially if you were to overdo it, you could permanently "stunt" the development of his marking ability. Instead of risking that, you should delay selection training until your dog is well along in triples.)

DRILL

Selection

Not too surprisingly, you begin teaching your dog to select in trial-and-success mode, by selecting on reruns only. In his initial run of a triple, you let him pick the marks up in whatever sequence he chooses. Then, when he is comfortable with all three marks, on a rerun, you send him for them in a different sequence. After he is comfortable with the concept, you gradually work selection into his regular work on triples.

Purpose of Drill

This drill teaches your dog to retrieve multiple marks in whatever sequence you choose.

Prerequisites

Your dog should be well along in triple marks, that is, doing good work on reasonably advanced tests.

Equipment and Facilities

This drill requires no special equipment or facilities—just what you normally use for triple marks.

Precautions and Pitfalls

Don't start this work too soon. If your dog is still wobbly on triples, wait. If you start too soon, you may damage the normal development of his marking skills.

Work on secondary selection first, and then add primary selection only after your dog is reasonably comfortable with that.

After you have trained him to select, don't overdo it. Do it in training only often enough to keep him comfortable with it. In trials and tests, use it only when it will reduce the probability that you will have to handle him on a mark.

Don't overwork your dog in any one session.

Process—Steps in Training

For a long time, you should limit your selecting to reruns, and then only after he has done a good job on a particular set of marks while retrieving them in his natural order. Start out with wide-spread, relatively simple triples, and with secondary selection. Then, as he progresses, mix in primary selection, but still with very basic tests, and only on reruns. You want him to succeed every time you select.

After he is comfortable with both secondary and primary selection in basic triples, you can safely work selecting into all his triples. Work on reruns only for a long, long time. Since you normally rerun him on any test he doesn't ace the first time, you can work on selecting without spending any extra time. Whenever you decide to rerun him to improve his marking, select on the rerun.

When should you start selecting on his initial runs? When his general deportment convinces you he can handle it. Even then, start out with widespread, very basic triples and with secondary selection. Gradually add primary selection to the mix, and make the tests more challenging.

Eventually, you can work selection into the initial runs of your normal training triples. *But don't overdo it!* Select just often enough to keep him comfortable with the idea, not so often that he becomes totally dependent on you.

Addenda

If you're training your retriever for hunting only, not with the intention of running him in dog-games, you don't really need to train him to select. In hunting, with only yourself to please, handling on an occasional mark will not be a problem. We justify selection in dog-games as sometimes necessary in order to present a dog's marking talents at their best. In dog-games we identify breeding stock, so poor marking is significantly penalized. Retrievers do two jobs: They mark and do blind retrieves. The blind retrieve is totally taught, not hereditary, but marking comes from the genes. Thus, in choosing retriever breeding stock, we should pay close attention to marking.

Appendix 1

Equipment

In the description of each drill, the necessary equipment is listed. Many of these items are used in several drills. Therefore, instead of describing them over and over there, I am describing all of them here in this Appendix, which you can use for reference as you go from drill to drill. In addition to the drill-specific items of equipment, I am also describing a few general pieces of equipment used throughout all phases of retriever training—whistles, lanyards, and so forth.

Belt Cord

This is a three- to four-foot length of stout cord with a loop on one end. It is useful in some of the preliminary drills (steadying and honoring). Ideally, you should make your belt cord from nylon, and burn both ends so they won't unravel. Attach the loop to your belt on your left side (assuming your dog heels on that side). To control your dog when he's sitting at heel, slip the other end of the belt cord under his strap collar and fold it back on itself. That way, you can restrain him with one hand by gripping the doubled-back end of the belt cord. When you release your grip, he can run right off of the belt cord, without even noticing that it's there. When you're not using it, you can wad your belt cord up and stuff it in your pocket, with the loop still attached to your belt.

A word of caution: If your dog's strap collar has a metal ring, do *not* slip the belt cord through it. If you do, as your dog departs, it may wrap up tightly around the metal ring. Twice retrievers have thusly removed important elements of my attire. Once my Chesapeake, Beaver,

161

ripped a piece out of a pair of my bib overalls. Another time my Golden, Deuce, unzipped my jeans and pulled them partway off—when a woman in the training group was standing nearby. I don't know which of us was more embarrassed. Needless to say, I've never put a belt cord through a metal ring on a dog's collar since then.

Birds

You will sometimes need birds for training. Mostly, you can get by with pigeons, but occasionally you will want gamebirds (ducks and pheasants). For training purposes, birds come in three "conditions": dead; clipped-wing; and live flier.

You can re-use dead birds many times before they must be discarded. Simply keep them in a freezer between uses. When you need them, thaw them out, use them, and then toss them back into the freezer. Like many retriever trainers, I have a special freezer in the garage for frozen birds. In it I keep pigeons, ducks, pheasants, and quail.

Clipped-wings, or more simply "clips," are live birds with the flight feathers pulled from one wing only. If you pull them from both wings, the bird will still be able to fly away. But if you pull them from only one wing, you throw the bird out of balance so he can only flutter and flop around. Mostly you'll use pigeons as clips.

Live fliers, of course, are live birds capable of flight. Again, you will normally use pigeons, but sometimes gamebirds come in handy.

Unless you plan to maintain your own "flock," you need a reliable bird supplier, someone who will sell you a few at a time. If you belong to a local retriever club, some of the members can direct you to a bird supplier. If your area has no retriever club, contact the nearest spaniel or pointing dog club. They need many more birds than do retriever trainers, so they have to have suppliers. If all else fails, talk to your veterinarian, who may be able to tell you who in your area raises birds as a hobby or as a business.

Blank Pistol

In a training group, you need a blank pistol mostly when you are throwing for someone else's dog. In fact, each person in the group should have one. The ideal blank pistol is one that fires shotshell primers, which are much cheaper than .22 blank shells and just as loud. To fire shotshell primers, a pistol must be center-fire, not rim-fire. Most of those in use today are .32 or .38 blank pistols that have been converted to primer usage through the insertion of a brass sleeve into each cylinder. These brass sleeves reduce the cylinder size to that of shotshell primers. A .22 pistol cannot be converted to primer usage because it is rim-fire.

Of course, a .22 blank pistol with regular .22 blank shells will do everything the primer pistol will do, but the ammunition will cost more. If you already have a .22 blank pistol, use it instead of buying another pistol for primers. Otherwise you would have to shoot thousands of rounds before you would break even.

Don't be tempted by the inexpensive little pistols that shoot .22 "crimp" shells. These shells don't make enough noise to be heard at any distance. They may be adequate for training pointing dogs, which are always very close to the shot. But for retrievers, where the distance between the dog and the thrower can be substantial, they just don't have enough bang.

Calls, Duck and Pheasant

For hunt tests, you should accustom your dog to the sound of duck and pheasant calls. In hunt tests, hidden gunners use them to attract the dog's attention before throwing marks. (The sounds that come from some of these calls in tests would terrorize any duck within earshot!) For a duck call, use whatever you use for hunting, or whatever you can find at the local sporting goods store. If, like most, you don't call pheasant . . . what next, pheasant decoys? . . . and therefore don't have a pheasant call, check with your local sporting goods store.

Collars

In general, there are three types of collars: chain, strap, and electronic. The chain training collar, often misnamed the "choke" collar, is an obedience training tool, so will not be specifically needed for any drill in this book (although it's ideal for obedience, especially the *Heel* command).

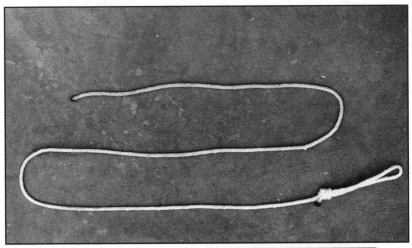

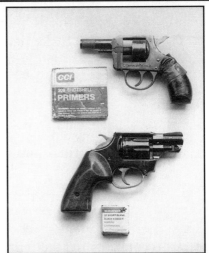

Above: Belt cord.

Right: Two blank pistols.

Below: Several duck calls.

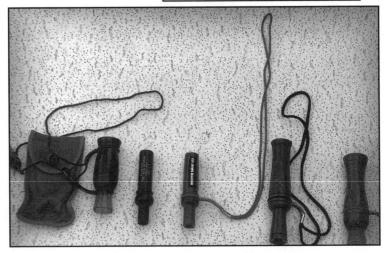

The strap collar has some usefulness in field work, especially during the steadying and honoring processes. (For this any flat strap collar will do, although leather doesn't work out too well for retrievers because of the water work.) Other than that, you should work your retriever without a collar, especially in water, where a collar can hang up on a snag and immobilize the dog.

The electronic collar (e-collar) is optional for some drills and necessary for others. If you prefer not to use an e-collar, you won't be able to use those drills for which it is necessary—unless you can invent another way to correct your dog immediately at a distance.

In Appendix II, you'll find all the information you need about e-collars and how to collar-condition your dog. Here I will only say that, if you

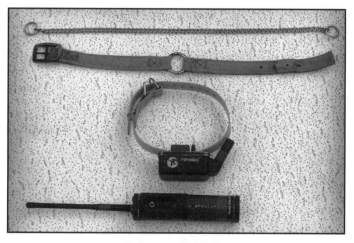

Three types of collars: top: chain training collar; middle: strap collar; bottom: electronic collar.

decide to get one, be sure to get one with variable levels of intensity, so you can adjust the amount of juice you give your dog to his particular tolerance level.

Dummies

You will need a goodly supply of dummies of one kind and another. The most generally useful are the small plastic knobbies. The white

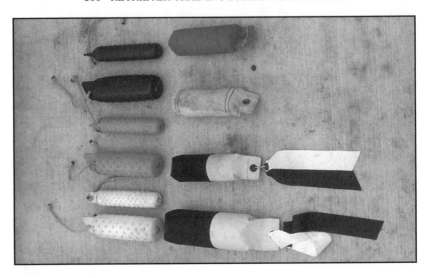

Assorted types of retrieving dummies.

ones are highly visible against dark backgrounds. The orange (or gray) ones are visible against light backgrounds. The black ones are visible against any background from light to medium dark. Frankly, the black ones are the most generally useful. In recent years, some companies have brought out two-tone, white and black, dummies that are visible against any background. The larger plastic knobbies also come in the same array of colors, and are useful in several situations.

Canvas dummies are also quite common. They come in a variety of sizes and colors. Some even have white and black ribbons on one end to simulate the flutter of a flying bird. I have many, many canvas dummies, and I use them, but not as often as I use the plastic knobbies. These latter can be thrown farther and more accurately, they retain their color better, and they generally last longer.

A word of caution: If you use canvas dummies, throw them away when they begin to deteriorate. I've seen more than one dog chew vigorously on rotting, leaking canvas dummies.

Lanyards

You will almost never see an experienced retriever trainer without a lanyard around his neck and two whistles dangling from said lanyard. I once saw a guy wearing his lanyard and whistles in an airport (and I have been

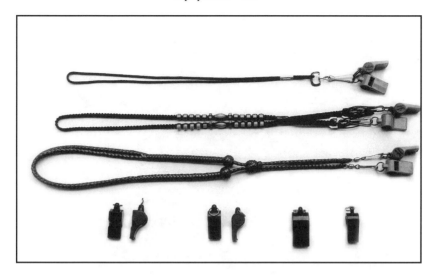

Assorted lanyards and whistles.

seen with mine in all sorts of places that have nothing to do with retriever training—grocery stores, restaurants, shopping malls, and so forth).

The lanyard keeps your whistles handy and free of the debris that can get into them if you carry them in your pocket. Lanyards come in many forms, from simple cords to elaborately braided leather affairs. In the psychedelic 1960s, and even into the mid-70s, retrieverites made a fad of wildly colored and heavily beaded macrame lanyards. Today, the more conservative braided leather type seems to be standard. Whatever your taste in lanyard design and construction, you should get one that accommodates two whistles—in case you blow the side out of one when you really need it. (If you didn't need a whistle at that moment, you wouldn't have blown the side out of one, would you?)

Leads

In general, three types of leads are useful to retriever trainers: slip-leads, standard four- to six-foot leads, and retractable leads.

The slip lead is a length of rope or leather with a loop on each end. By running one end through the loop on the other end, you can make a makeshift collar for your dog. Using the loop on the other end as a hand-hold (like on a "normal" lead), you have a one-piece "traffic lead," which is ideal for heeling your dog to and from the line, and so forth. A slip-

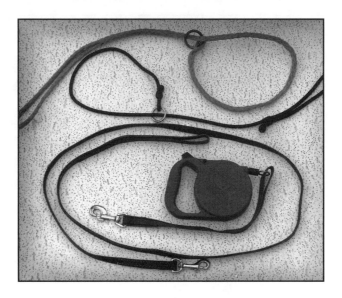

Four leads. At top, a slip-lead made from nylon rope; next, a
slip-lead made of braided leather; next, a six-foot leather lead;
within the six-foot lead is a retractable lead.

lead needn't be longer than four feet, and many of them are three feet or
less. Being rope or leather, it can be rolled up and stuffed in a pocket
when not needed. Rope slip-leads are inexpensive, especially if you make
them yourself (as I do) from nylon rope. Leather slip-leads, especially the
braided ones with matching lanyards, are quite expensive. Frankly, I use
these fancy leather ones only on spaniels and pointing dogs, because
retrievers are too often wet when I want to put a slip-lead on them.

The standard four- to six-foot lead, made of webbing or strap leather,
has a snap on one end and a hand-loop on the other. They are handy for
many things—obedience training, "airing" your dog in public places,
going for walks with your dog, and so on—so everyone should have one
(and most of us have accumulated several over the years).

The retractable lead offers you a slick way to control your dog on a
long line. It has an automatic reel that lets line out and brings it in as the
dog goes away from and comes toward you. It has a button with which
you can stop him and hold him at any fixed distance. It's chief benefit is
that your dog seldom tangles the long line around his legs . . . or yours.
For retrievers, I use a large retractable lead, with about twenty-six feet of
line

Two different brands of two-way radios.   Gary Corbin looks through a range-finder.

Radios, Two-Way

Although not absolutely necessary, having radio communications with your throwers can be handy. Some dogs get spooky when the boss yells instructions to a thrower. With little two-way radios, you can speak in a normal voice and be heard at a great distance.

Range-Finder

To determine how far away a given mark or blind is, or to set one up at a given distance, you have three choices: estimate it, step it off, or use a range-finder. Most of us don't estimate too accurately. Stepping distances off takes time, and can't be done in water work. *Ergo*, if precise distances matter to you, you need a range-finder.

Remote Dummy Launchers—Single-Shot

In recent year, several firms have manufactured electronically-controlled remote launchers that will throw dummies or birds just like a human assistant (only more consistently). They look like huge sling-shots that use surgical tubing for power. Since they use a pouch for the "projectile," they can throw either dummies or birds. (I call them

Diane O'Hearne demonstrates the "Training Group" single-shot remote dummy launcher, which is made by Wahiakum Enterprises and operated remotely with Tri-Tronics electronics. Several other companies make similar machines, which are operated by various electronic devices. All such devices can launch either dummies or birds.

"dummy launchers" to distinguish them from the remote bird launchers described below.) This slingshot type launcher is a "single-shot" device, so must be reloaded for each throw. The resulting delay between runs can disrupt the rhythm of some drills.

However, if you must train alone, these launchers can be most helpful. You can set such a launcher up where your assistant would stand, bring your dog to the line, and impulse the launcher to throw the

Two makes of multi-shot remote dummy launchers. On the left is a four-shot "Bumper Boy," which is powered by .22 blank shells, operated remotely by Bumper Boy electronics, and has various warning sounds (duck call, shot, human voice, and so forth), plus a silhouette (of a young woman) which can be attached to the top to simulate a bird thrower. On the right is five-shot "Max 5000," which is powered by a mixture of gases and operated remotely by Tri-Tronics electronics. Either machine can launch multiple dummies without being reloaded each time, but neither can launch birds. Other firms make functionally similar units, powered various ways and operated remotely by various electronic devices.

dummy or bird by pushing on your transmitter button. By using two or three launchers controlled by the same transmitter, you can set up the same double and triple marks you can with two or three assistants to throw for you.

These remote launchers are quite expensive, but if you have to train alone, they may well be worth the price.

Remote Dummy Launchers—Multi-Shot

More recently, a few companies have produced multi-shot remote dummy launchers powered by blank shells or gas. These are small, platform-like devices on which you mount several dummies. With the transmitter, you can fire the dummies one at a time from a distance. This facilitates repetitive drilling, because you don't have to reload the

A remote bird launcher. This is a Tri-Tronics model, operated remotely by Tri-Tronics electronics. Several other firms make similar pieces of equipment, operated remotely by various electronics devices.

launcher after every retrieve. With two or three of them, you can set up the same double and triple marks you can set up with two or three assistants to throw for you, and you don't have to reload after every run.

These, too, are quite expensive. However, if you must train alone, they allow you to simulate a training group situation.

Remote Bird Launchers

Retriever trainers have also improvised with remote bird launchers developed long ago for pointing dog trainers. These are small, box-like, spring-loaded devices that flip a bird up in the air, but not too vigorously. Retriever trainers have made limited use of them, especially in the "pop-up" blind. Although cheaper than the Remote Dummy Launchers, described above, they "still ain't cheap."

More recently, some firms are producing more powerful remote bird launchers specifically for retrievers. These look much like the pointing breed launchers, but they throw the bird or dummy much farther. This makes them suitable for throwing marks.

Shotguns

Whenever you need a shotgun in any of these drills (normally for shooting fliers), use whatever weapon you use for waterfowl and/or upland gamebird hunting.

Sit-Stick

This is the canine name for what horse folks call a "riding crop." It is useful for correcting the dog when he is heeling improperly, when his line manners leave something to be desired, and so on. It is not specifically required in any drill in this book, but it is a handy tool to have around whenever you heel your dog off-lead.

The secret of using a sit-stick effectively is to pet your dog with it much more often than you correct him with it. If you use it only for corrections, he will fear it and shy away from it. If you pet him with it often, especially when he is sitting at heel, he won't learn to fear it, even after you correct him with it. If you decide to use a sit-stick, carry it with you constantly while training your dog and pet him with it—*a lot*.

Squirt Bottle

This is a plastic bottle with a small nozzle and trigger built into the cap. With it, you can send a stream of water into your dog's face when the occasion calls for it. I use one of these around home, mostly to teach and reinforce the *Hush* command when my dogs get noisy in their kennels. It is also useful in dealing with dogs that are noisy on the line while working.

You can buy these in several sizes at any lawn and garden store. I use the one-pint size, because it fits so nicely into one of the front bird pockets of my training vest.

On left, a white traffic cone visual aid; on right, a black and white flag visual aid elevated on a short orange stake; in the middle, three stakes (a tall orange one, a middle-sized orange one, and a tall white one).

Stakes

I use stakes in two colors, orange and white, and in a variety of sizes. Since dogs are color-blind, they don't notice orange stakes (unless they stand up too high above the cover). So I use orange stakes to mark blind retrieve dummy piles. That way, I know where the pile is, but my

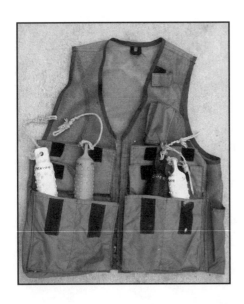

A training vest, with retrieving dummies inserted in some of the pockets to show where they are. In the back, this vest has a full-sized game bag. This vest was made by Wick. Other firms make similar vests.

dog doesn't. I also use orange stakes to elevate my visual aids when I use them in cover. I sometimes use white stakes as visual aids, especially when I want the dog to run for a distance before he sees it.

I make my stakes from inch and a quarter wood dowel and long guttering spikes. I drill a hole in one end of the stake, and drive the guttering spike into the hole. Then I cut off the head of the guttering spike so I can stick it into the ground easily. I also drill a somewhat larger hole in the other end of the stake, so I can stack them to make a taller stake when I need it. Also, to elevate my white and black flags above the cover, I stick the little "flag pole" into the hole in the top of a stake. I make my stakes in several lengths, from about 12 inches to about 36 inches.

Vest

When you train a retriever, you often must tote a lot of equipment —dummies and birds, collars and leads, blank pistols and shells, shotgun shells, the transmitter for electronic equipment (e-collar, remote dummy launchers), and so forth. For some strange reason, retriever trainers in general haven't yet figured out what spaniel and pointing dog trainers have known for decades, namely, that a multi-pocketed vest is ideal for hauling all this paraphernalia around.

I have long used an orange spaniel/birddog training vest for retriever training. It has pockets for everything I normally carry, with extra pockets left over most of the time. This vest frees up both of my hands and eliminates the need to drop things on the ground (and then search for them later). It also facilitates moving from place to place, like when lengthening a drill out or when throwing dummies for someone else in the "walking marks" drill.

I have encountered one very slight problem with it. When standing still for long periods, as in throwing dummies for someone else, I've found that bumblebees mistake my orange vest for a huge flower! They will home in on it from incredible distances. However, when they get close to me, they realize their mistake and leave. I've never had one sting me, or even light on me, but I have given any number of them a lot of exercise. To eliminate this distraction, my wife made me a blue denim vest patterned after my orange one. So far, the bumblebees have not "decoyed" to it like they did the orange one. If you train only retrievers, and want a vest, you should opt for a dull-colored one.

Visual Aids

In blind retrieve training, you will use visual aids to indicate to your dog where the dummy piles are. For many years, I used and advocated little white cones—orange traffic cones either painted white or covered with sleeves of white cloth. More recently, I've switched to little white and black flags. Other trainers use white plastic crates, white paint buckets, and heaven only knows what else. I've heard that a trainer in Colorado makes and uses little white "teepees" from three stakes and white cloth. They look like cones, but are much lighter and handier.

Whistles

You should have two identical whistles dangling from your lanyard, and they should be plastic rather than metal. In cold weather, metal whistles will freeze to your lips and then peel the skin off when you remove the whistle from your mouth. Some whistles have peas and some don't. Those with peas trill very nicely, but they freeze up and don't work in cold weather. For years I used the Roy Gonia (with a pea) in warm weather and the Fox (without a pea) in cold weather. Then the Gonia whistle came out in two configurations, one with and the other without a pea. I switched to the latter and use it year around. (Some more inventive types removed the pea from the old Gonias with a razor blade. I wasn't that bright.)

People tend to become emotional about their choice of whistles. When I started in retrievers, the Acme Thunderer was *the* whistle. Everyone who was anyone in retrievers used it, especially among the pros. I tried it, but didn't like it as well as I liked the Gonia, so I used the Gonia, and struggled to survive in an Acme Thunderer world. Today it's a Gonia world, and looking back I find it hard to believe that I received so much unsolicited advice about my poor choice of whistles. When my dogs messed up, I was told it wasn't a lack of training; no, it was that I wasn't using a "proper" Acme Thunderer whistle! Today the opposite might happen. If I were to wear anything but a Gonia, those given to offering unsolicited advice would attribute any problem I might have with a dog to the fact that I wasn't using a Gonia whistle.

The point is: Use the whistle you like best, and train your dog to respond to it, and all will be well with you.

Appendix 2

The Electronic Collar

For the typical beginner, the electronic collar, or e-collar, looms as something mysterious, intimidating, and more than a little controversial. Thus it deserves separate coverage in this Appendix. To de-mystify it, and to clarify its position in retriever training, let's review the following areas: the controversy surrounding it; what it can and cannot do; and how to introduce a dog to it. After studying all that information, you should be able to make an intelligent—and, I hope, unemotional—decision about whether to use the e-collar.

Let me start off by confessing that I strongly favor the *modern* e-collar when used with the *modern* training techniques which have been developed for it, principally by Jim Dobbs. More on both of these later.

The Controversy

The e-collar, which came into relatively widespread use in the 1960s, has been surrounded by controversy throughout its short history. And, like all controversies, this one has been highly emotional. Some proclaim the e-collar as the greatest single piece of training equipment in the history of dogdom. Others damn it as an instrument of torture, a device too brutal to be used on man's best friend. Most fall somewhere between these extremes.

Quite frankly, the early e-collars were crude affairs. They had only one level of stimulation: maximum. They had only one type of stimulation: continuous. And they were not too reliable. I'll probably never forget the nightmare I witnessed years ago when my training buddy's

177

collar wouldn't turn off. His dog was on the other side of a small lake. He zapped the dog for some error or another, but when he let off on the button, the electricity did *not* stop—which was apparent from the way the poor dog contorted and wailed on the far shore. My buddy had to jump in his car, drive around the lake, and take the collar off his dog. All that time, I could hear the animal's pathetic howling, and I could see him writhing in agony. As I said, I'm not apt to forget that episode.

Nor am I apt to forget the dogs I saw back in the early days that were ruined by misuse of those early models. Because almost every pro used one, the e-collar became a status symbol among amateurs. Consequently, many clueless souls bought e-collars, proudly strapped them on their dogs, and used them in totally nonintelligent (= stupid) ways. Whenever the dog did anything even slightly wrong, the boss held the transmitter button down until he, the boss, felt vindicated. I saw dogs refuse to come out of their crates voluntarily. I saw dogs crawl on their bellies whenever they had the e-collar around their necks.

The Modern E-Collar

But why go on? The point is: I favor the *modern* e-collar in spite of what I have seen done with earlier models, especially by nonintelligent "trainers." I favor it because the *modern* e-collar differs radically from its predecessors, and because at least one *modern* training program for the e-collar is absolutely humane. True, improper use of even the best of modern e-collars will still ruin a dog. But today, anyone who will put in a little time and effort can learn how to use the e-collar in a program that is quite gentle, and much more effective than anything else currently available.

The major advancement in today's e-collars over the early ones is "variable levels of stimulation." The old collars had only the maximum level, which was a hefty jolt. Dogs, like people, vary in their sensitivity to electric shock, so in the early days of the e-collar many—in fact most—dogs were significantly overstimulated, day after day. Today, the trainer can select levels of stimulation that range from almost imperceptible to maximum. He can adjust the amount of juice he uses to the sensitivity of his particular dog. No dog need ever be stimulated beyond his tolerance level.

A second advancement in the modern collar is selectable "momentary" and "continuous" stimulation. In momentary mode, when the trainer pushes the button, the dog is stimulated for only an instant (perhaps a millisecond) no matter how long the trainer holds the button down. Many training situations are best handled with momentary stimulation. (In the drill descriptions of this book, whenever I recommend momentary stimulation, I say you should "nick" your dog with the e-collar.) In continuous mode, the dog is stimulated as long as the trainer holds the transmitter button down, up to a maximum of 10 seconds when an automatic cutoff takes over on most collars. (Would that my training buddy's collar had been so equipped that day he couldn't turn it off!) Many training situations are best handled with continuous stimulation. (In the drill descriptions of this book, whenever I recommend continuous stimulation, I say you should "zap" your dog with the e-collar.) Some collars have only one mode, either momentary or continuous. I would recommend a collar with both, but if you have a collar with only one, you can simulate the other mode fairly well. If yours is a momentary-only collar, you can push and release the transmitter button repeatedly and rapidly to simulate continuous stimulation. If you have a continuous-only collar, you can tap and release the transmitter button to simulate momentary stimulation. But these are make-do techniques. If possible, you should get a collar that allows you to select either mode as you need it.

Today's e-collars have several other optional features, most of which you can live without. Some have a "praise tone" button, which allows you to whisper sweet nothings in your dog's ear at a distance (after appropriate training in what this tone means). Having a good set of lungs, I'd rather yell "Good dog!" than spend the time it takes to teach the dog what this praise tone means. Some e-collars have a warning tone that sounds immediately before stimulation. Frankly, on the early high-voltage-only collars, this was a faltering first step toward variable stimulation. The theory was that, after regularly hearing this warning tone immediately before stimulation, the dog would react to the sound itself, and obey without being juiced, at least some of the time. That was a good idea when every push of the transmitter button lit the dog up like a Christmas tree, but variable stimulation has made it purposeless. This dinosaur may have a place in the Smithsonian, but not on modern e-collars. If it is automatic—incapable of being turned off—it's worse than useless, for it prevents you from determining the proper level of stimulation for your particular dog. At every stimulation level, he will react to the sound, so you won't be able to tell when he first notices the electricity. Frankly, I wouldn't have a collar with this feature, unless I could turn it off, and leave it off.

In summary, if you are planning to buy an e-collar, your first priority should be for variable levels of stimulation. Secondly, if possible, you should get a collar with selectable momentary and continuous stimulation modes. Beyond that, suit your fancy.

What the E-Collar Can Do

The e-collar allows you to send a negative message to your dog immediately at any reasonable distance. Since the timing of corrections is so critical in dog training, and since the distances in retriever training can be great, this tool fulfills a big need. No wonder pros persisted in using the early models, which had so many drawbacks!

But the e-collar is not a magic do-all training device. It has no special magic. As a matter of fact, it has only two uses.

First, the e-collar allows you to enforce *known* commands. If your dog is deliberately disobeying, especially at a distance, you can send him an "e-mail" correction immediately, while he is still in the act of disobeying. However, for this to be effective, he must understand what he should be doing. Thus, he must have already been trained to obey a given command before you can correct him for disobeying it with the e-collar. The advantage of the e-collar over, say, a swat with a newspaper or any other such correction, is that the e-collar "swats" him immediately even when he's beyond the reach of your newspaper.

Second, the e-collar enables you to create geographical "hot-spots" for your dog at a distance. A "hot-spot" is a place you want your dog to avoid. Dogs are highly place-conscious relative to punishment. They avoid places in which they have been punished. In fact, the more severely they have been punished in a place, the longer they avoid it. Thank heaven for this trait! Without it, I don't know how we would teach retrievers certain things, like switch-proofing, suction-proofing, angled water entries, and so forth. If your dog goes somewhere he shouldn't— like detouring to an island when he should swim straight past it—you can turn that island into a hot-spot by nicking him with the e-collar as soon as he lands on it. Then, on the rerun he will stay away from that island, and take the line you give him.

What the E-Collar Can *Not* Do

The e-collar is the finest long-distance correction and hot-spotting tool available today, but it is not a *training* tool. You cannot *teach* your dog anything with it. You must teach him through other methods. Only then can you use the e-collar to correct him for related disobedience.

If he doesn't know what he is supposed to do before you push the transmitter button, he won't know afterwards either. The only exception to that rule is hot-spotting. Keep that in mind, and you'll never abuse your dog with the e-collar.

Collar-Conditioning

Before you can use the e-collar for its primary purpose, namely, to re-enforce commands your dog already understands, you must "collar-condition" him. That means you must help him make the association between your commands and electricity from the collar. You can best do this in the backyard, with his basic obedience commands—*Sit*, *Heel*, *Come-in*, *Kennel*, and so on—which he already understands. (If you haven't obedience-trained him yet, neither of you is yet ready for the e-collar!) After making the proper association on several such commands, your dog will generalize the meaning of electricity. Then you can use the collar to re-enforce any command he understands.

Step 1: The Bark Collar

Although it isn't absolutely necessary, you should, if possible, first introduce your dog to electricity with an electronic bark collar. It will zap him whenever he barks. It won't take him long to figure out that he can stop the zapping by stopping the noise, and that he can prevent it altogether by being quiet when he feels like barking. That is a solid psychological foundation for "collar-conditioning," in which you teach him to turn off the juice by obeying a command and to prevent the juice by obeying promptly.

Starting out with a bark collar also works him through any trauma electricity may initially induce. He will learn to accept it as the normal result of barking. Thus he won't freak out when you first hit the transmitter button on the regular e-collar.

Frankly, there is one more reason for starting with the bark collar, although most trainers are reluctant to mention it. After being pre-conditioned with a bark collar, a dog won't vocalize when stimulated with the regular e-collar. Some dogs that haven't been pre-conditioned this way wail piteously at the slightest electrical impulse. Such a dog makes his trainer look like a monster even if he isn't overstimulating the beast. Let's face it: Some dogs are more prone to vocalize than others. It's in the genes. But we can overcome this particular gene with the bark collar.

Step 2: Determining the Proper Level of Stimulation

Before you can properly collar-condition your dog, you must determine his sensitivity to electricity. Dogs, like people, can tolerate varying degrees of shock. My wife is so sensitive to it that she is afraid to replace a burned-out light bulb. At the other extreme, I once knew a man who said that letting small currents flow through him relaxed him. He would stand for several seconds touching two electrically operated machines that gave him this sensation. I touched them accidentally once and jumped away at the first jolt of juice. Dogs also have different tolerances, and you should find the lowest level your dog clearly notices, the lowest level to which he reacts. He may twitch his ears or head. He may look surprised. He may glance around. But he will tell you in some way when you have found the lowest level he notices.

Put the e-collar on him and let him run around the backyard wearing it long enough so he no longer notices the additional weight. Now put him on lead, but not on command. Were he on command, he might not react noticeably when he should. Give him a continuous stimulation with the lowest level your collar offers. (If you have a momentary-only collar, tap the button repeatedly.) If he doesn't react in any way, move up to the next higher level, and so on, until he lets you know that he feels the electricity. That is his "base" level of stimulation. In some training situations, especially when he's either highly distracted or strongly determined to disobey, you may have to use a higher level to "communicate" with him. However, for most training, you should use his base level.

Step 3: Sit!

Having determined your dog's sensitivity to the e-collar, you can begin collar-conditioning him with his basic obedience commands. Start out with *Sit*. Put him on lead, wearing the e-collar. Let him move around near you. Then start continuous stimulation immediately *before* commanding *Sit*. Since he already understands the command, he will plop his posterior down. As soon as he does, discontinue stimulation, and praise him. You want him to learn that he can turn the juice off by

Collar-conditioning. Gary Corbin reinforces the *Sit* command with the e-collar. His dog is "Ben" (Benden's Xcalibur JH WC).

obeying. Thus, you hold the button down until he has obeyed, by sitting in this case. Why did you start stimulation before giving the command? Had you waited until afterwards, he might have thought he was being zapped for obeying the command. But with the electricity starting before the command, he won't misunderstand.

Repeat this several times, until he starts to sit when you start stimulation, even before you can say *Sit*. When he reacts that quickly, you know he understands how to turn the juice off. From then on, say *Sit* first, and only zap him when he is slow in responding. In subsequent training sessions, surprise him with the *Sit* command or the *Sit*-whistle—while he is heeling, while he is coming to you on command, even while he is romping around. Anytime he disobeys or even obeys too slowly, push the transmitter button and hold it down until he is sitting.

Within a few sessions, he will have mastered how to turn off—in fact, how to avoid—the electricity when you say *Sit* or blow the *Sit*-whistle. Then, you can move on to the next obedience command, *Come-in!*

Step 4: Come-in!

Follow the same procedure with this command. With him on lead and wearing the e-collar, put him on a *Sit-Stay* command and walk to the end of the (six-foot) lead. Start stimulation immediately before you toot the *Come-in* whistle. So far, in his mind, stimulation has always meant for him to *Sit*, so he may refuse to budge. To help him overcome this hang-up, pull him gently toward you with the lead, and sweet-talk him as he approaches. Turn off the juice as soon as he is moving toward you.

Repeat this several times, until he begins to get up when you start stimulation, without waiting for the command or whistle. Now he thinks stimulation means he should get up and start toward you. He may even think that it no longer means *Sit*. So you must disabuse him of that little misconception. Start mixing up the *Sit* and *Come-in* commands (or whistles) in each session. Whenever he disobeys either one, or is even slow in obeying, zap him with the e-collar. After a few sessions, he will figure out that electricity can mean either *Sit* or *Come-in*, whichever you happened to have said last. That is his first step toward generalizing the meaning of collar stimulation.

Step 5: Kennel!

Next, follow the same procedure with the command *Kennel!* For this, you can use either his kennel run or a crate. Start immediately in front of the gate or door. Initially, you should run a rope from your dog through the length of the run or crate and have an assistant at the far end hold the other end of the rope, ready to guide your dog with the rope as needed. Optionally, you can double the rope back around some fixed object behind the run or crate and handle the rope yourself. Start stimulation, then command *Kennel*. Your assistant, or you yourself, should then use the rope to guide your dog into the run or crate. As soon as he gets there, stop stimulation and praise him.

Repeat this until you no longer need the rope, that is, until he heads for his kennel or crate as soon as he feels stimulation. Thereafter, don't stimulate him unless he disobeys or is slow in obeying. Once he has the concept, start backing farther and farther away from the run or crate before telling him to *Kennel*.

Of course, to help him understand that electricity has no single fixed meaning, you should also work him on *Sit* and *Come-in* while you are going through the *Kennel* step. When he has mastered all three—*Sit, Come-in,* and *Kennel*—you have collar-conditioned him on three totally different, seemingly contradictory commands. You can correct him for disobedience to any of them with the e-collar, and he will

Collar-conditioning. Gary Corbin reinforces the *Come-in* command with the e-collar.

Collar-conditioning. Gary Corbin reinforces the *Kennel* command with the e-collar.

understand what he has to do to turn off the juice. At this point, your dog is "in balance," to use Jim Dobbs' term. With the proper command and appropriate stimulation, he will stop, go, or come. For all practical purposes, he has generalized his understanding of the meaning of e-collar stimulation, and you can proceed to use it to enforce any command at any reasonable distance.

Step 6: Et Cetera, Et Cetera, Et Cetera

However, for insurance, you should collar-condition your dog to other commands, too, for example, *Heel*. Follow the same steps as you have with *Sit*, *Come-in*, and *Kennel*. This will not only help your dog generalize collar stimulation, but it will help you get your dog from your vehicle to the line, or duck blind, in good order.

If you have already force-broken your dog, you should also introduce the e-collar to enforce *Fetch* and *Give*. This will give you a very solid basis for dealing with the three infamous mouth problems covered in Chapter 3: hardmouth, stickiness, and sloppy-mouth.

Step 7: Hot-Spotting

Technically, using the e-collar to create hot-spots (which the dog will avoid) requires no formal conditioning steps, beyond accustoming the dog to electricity with the electronic bark collar. However, in actual practice, you should *not* use your e-collar for hot-spotting before collar-conditioning him with the above procedure. If you intend to use the e-collar for both purposes, as most of us do, you should collar-condition him before using it for either purpose.

ADDENDA

The above approach to collar-conditioning—and the ways I suggest you use the e-collar throughout this book—follows the Dobbs' program, which I use and recommend. However, I should mention another program that is very popular today. I'll call it the "field trial program."

This program has been developed by highly successful field trial pros. Most dogs that are winning and placing in field trials today have achieved their success through this program. It is unequaled in its ability to instill field-trial precision in a retriever. In the hands of a cool-headed, experienced trainer who consistently reads dogs correctly, it is unbeatable. Thus, if you are such a trainer, and especially if you intend to compete in the major stakes at field trials, I recommend that you learn and use this program.

However, if you are not cool-headed, or not experienced, or not able to consistently read dogs correctly—in other words if you are the typical hunter and hunt-test participant for whom I'm writing this book—I recommend that you stick with the Dobbs' program.

In the field trial program, you don't use the lowest level of juice your dog notices. Instead you use the highest level he can tolerate without folding. Most who follow this program use the highest level their collars can put out. To offset this voltage, they use the e-collar much more sparingly than do those who follow the Dobbs' program. To minimize e-collar usage, they use several alternative techniques. Frequently, they handle their dogs (*a la* blind retrieve) to keep them on line to marks as well as blinds. Sometimes they use what they call "attrition," which means that they repeat disobeyed commands, thereby giving the dog additional chances to correct himself. Sometimes they use what they call "indirect pressure," in which they stop the dog, then before repeating the disobeyed command, they give him a "wake-up call" nick with the e-collar. And so on. Clearly, the trainer must be cool-headed, experienced, and capable of reading dogs accurately to make consistently appropriate decisions about when to use the e-collar and when to rely on one of these alternative techniques—and, for that matter, which one of those to use in any given situation.

For such a person, especially if he wants to win field trials, this program is unbeatable. However, since every push on the transmitter button gives the dog all the juice the collar is capable of delivering, every mistake is a serious mistake. And even the best field trial trainers occasionally misread a situation and "burn" their dogs when they shouldn't. Can you imagine how often the inexperienced trainer who seldom reads his dog correctly would burn his dog in error? Worse still, how about the hot-headed individual?

I've seen such amateurs—those who lack the prerequisite temperament, experience, and canine insight—abuse this program. It wasn't a pretty picture, believe me. That's why I cannot recommend it. On the other hand, if you make mistakes with the minimal juice used in the Dobbs' program, your mistakes will be small ones. Thus, I feel comfortable in recommending it. Granted, with the Dobbs' program, a person probably cannot achieve the same field trial precision that top pros achieve with the field trial program. But, who needs it? Hunters certainly don't. Hunt testers certainly *shouldn't*. If hunt tests ever so mimic field trials that participants must follow the field trial e-collar program, hunt tests will have failed in their primary purpose, namely, to provide an avenue where ordinary dog-owning hunters can succeed with their personally trained dogs.

Ergo, the people for whom I'm writing this book don't need the precision the field trial e-collar program offers. Nor are most of them capable of using such a high-risk program effectively.

Enough said.

Index of Drills

You'll want to read these, too . . .

Training Retrievers for Marshes and Meadows
James B. Spencer

Spencer's basic text on training for the amateur. A complete training manual that guides you step by step through:
- Getting acquainted with your puppy and starting him off right
- Basic obedience exercises every Retriever needs to know
- Teaching your dog single marked retrieves
- Training double marked retrieves
- Doing advanced marks and blinds
- Training your dog to do blind retrieves.

Softcover, ISBN 1-57779-007-3

Retriever Training Tests
James B. Spencer

The first book ever to concentrate on the environment the retriever must work in and how it affects the dog's training and work. Spencer explains which environmental factors are significant and why. Prepare you dog for successful hunting tests. Get this book today.

Softcover, ISBN 0-931866-95-2

Retriever Puppy Training
Clarice Rutherford and Cherylon Loveland

Is your retriever your house pet, and also your hunting companion? Yes, he can be both — the authors tell you how to raise your puppy successfully in this scenario. A unique feature is a section on the personality traits of retrievers and how to adjust your training accordingly.
- Select the right puppy
- What to do with your puppy between six and sixteen week of age
- Start early by making retrieving fun
- Learn lots of yard work exercises to do at home
- Beginning field work — when and how.

Softcover, ISBN 0-931866-38-3

Retriever Training Drills for Blind Retrieves   Softcover, ISBN 1-57779-033-2
Retriever Training Drills for Marking   Softcover, ISBN 1-57779-032-4

Look for these and other fine Alpine titles at your local bookseller, or you may order direct from the publisher at 1-800-777-7257 or by writing to Alpine Publications, P. O. Box 7027, Loveland, CO 80537. For the latest information and prices check our website: www.AlpinePub.com.